Libraries, Archives, and Museums Today

Libraries, Archives, and Museums Today

Insights from the Field

Peter Botticelli
Martha R. Mahard
Michèle V. Cloonan

ROWMAN & LITTLEFIELD
Lanham • Boulder • New York • London

Published by Rowman & Littlefield
An imprint of The Rowman & Littlefield Publishing Group, Inc.
4501 Forbes Boulevard, Suite 200, Lanham, Maryland 20706
www.rowman.com

6 Tinworth Street, London SE11 5AL, United Kingdom

British Library Cataloguing in Publication Information Available

Library of Congress Cataloging-in-Publication Data

Names: Botticelli, Peter, 1966–, author. | Mahard, Martha R., 1948–, author. | Cloonan, Michèle Valerie, 1955–, author.
Title: Libraries, archives, and museums today : insights from the field / [edited by] Peter Botticelli, Martha R. Mahard, Michèle V. Cloonan.
Description: Lanham : Rowman & Littlefield, [2019] | Includes bibliographical references and index.
Identifiers: LCCN 2018044287 (print) | LCCN 2018057387 (ebook) | ISBN 9781538125564 (Electronic) | ISBN 9781538125540 (cloth : alk. paper) | ISBN 9781538125557 (pbk. : alk. paper)
Subjects: LCSH: Information services—Management—Case studies. | Collection management (Libraries)—Case studies. | Archives—Collection management—Case studies. | Museums—Collection management—Case studies. | Electronic information resources—Management—Case studies.
Classification: LCC ZA3157 (ebook) | LCC ZA3157 .L53 2019 (print) | DDC 025.1—dc23
LC record available at https://lccn.loc.gov/2018044287

∞ ™ The paper used in this publication meets the minimum requirements of American National Standard for Information Sciences Permanence of Paper for Printed Library Materials, ANSI/NISO Z39.48-1992.

Printed in the United States of America

Contents

Foreword

This book tackles one of the most debated issues in the recent history of collecting institutions: convergence. To what extent are libraries, archives, and museums (LAMs) converging in the digital age? How much convergence is desirable? What does convergence mean, anyway? The *Oxford English Dictionary* defines convergence as a "coming or drawing together" and "movement directed toward or terminating in the same point," which suggests that, for LAMs, convergence might not result in actual mergers between institutions. Instead, it could mark a drawing together of the operating methods and types of systems used by LAMs, something that makes a good deal of sense in the digital age. Indeed, in 2002 the *OED* added a new definition for convergence: "the process by which originally distinct technologies may become more compatible or integrated as they develop," leading to devices that are increasingly "multifunctional and interoperable."[1] With the history of technology convergence in mind, as long ago as the 1980s some computer scientists anticipated the disappearance of physical libraries and the merging of heritage collections online.[2]

However, the idea of a full convergence or integration of LAMs has never taken hold. This partly reflects the history of digitization efforts by LAMs, which began as "boutique" projects, with institutions seeking to digitize prestigious collections and those already in high demand by scholars. This small-scale approach, with a focus on digital access through institutional websites, initially served to reproduce the institutional boundaries around LAM repositories, forcing users to navigate from one local website to another in search of relevant information. But just as digital devices have moved toward convergence in their design, the past decade or so has seen the rise of new forces driving convergence in the LAM sector. A big change came in 2004, with the launch of the Google Books Library Project.[3] Even with copyright being a major limiting factor, Google's scanning effort opened the floodgates to mass digitization, not only of books but also of manuscripts, archival materials, and museum collections, along with associated documentation. More recently, as the scale of digital assets owned by LAMs has continued to grow, we have seen the emergence of aggregator services at the regional, national (e.g., DPLA), and international (e.g., Europeana Internet Archive) levels. These efforts reflect the underlying value of interoperability in access systems and in the methods for documenting, accessing, and experiencing cultural heritage collections online. As we look back to the early days of the digital revolution, it is clear that LAMs have found online audiences for just about anything and everything in their collections, essentially confirming Chris Anderson's 2004 observation about the "long tail" of demand for digital content.[4]

Certainly, there are more reasons for collaboration among libraries, archives, and museums of all types and sizes today than before the digital era, when collections lived exclusively in physical silos. Funding agencies such as the Institute of Museum and Library Services (IMLS) in the U.S. have played an important role in advancing local digitization efforts for LAM repositories, and they have also invested directly in collaborative projects that cut across disciplines and institutional boundaries to promote good practices and shared protocols. IMLS and others have worked actively to establish robust models for digital curation using common technologies and standards; such efforts have led to real advances in digital access and preservation. And yet, while many institutions have embraced collaboration as a practical means to share technology resources and expertise, LAMs have often been hesitant to cede control of digital resources to third parties, since information professions value the ability to control material objects as a central part of their mission.

In looking back on the experience of LAMs in the early digital age, it is not hard to find signs of convergence. Yet it is also clear that projects, collections, and institutions are all different, and this diversity is a source of strength as well as a challenge for those seeking to advance technology and promote collaboration between LAMs. This book advances our understanding of the complex issues behind convergence by offering a rich set of case studies that highlight the uniqueness of LAMs while exploring points of commonality between them. For the authors, the use of case studies has grown out of the immediate pedagogical need to give students practical examples of strategies that have worked well in the field and what has not gone so well as institutions adapt to the new demands of the digital age. The range of institutions, and institutional types, explored here make this book particularly valuable to students as well as working professionals in all types of LAMs. The book also reflects the authors' decades of experience as practitioners, as well as in teaching and conducting research in the fields of art documentation, cultural heritage preservation, and digital curation.

It is possible to imagine a point, however distant, at which data collections of all kinds can be discovered, understood, and used by researchers, students, cultural heritage professionals, and the general public for any reason at any time. At the same time, these data objects will need to accurately reflect their origins and context (provenance, in the widest sense of the term) so as not to lose their meaning. This will require ongoing efforts to communicate and work across disciplinary and professional lines. The conversation on convergence is likely to continue for the foreseeable future, and the potential for convergence of data collections is a goal worth pursuing. At the same time, the uniqueness of each profession and the reasons for its distinctive vision and mission must be preserved to allow the voice of each community to continue to be heard.

Joyce Ray, program coordinator and senior lecturer for the Johns Hopkins University Certificate in Digital Curation Program and former associate deputy for library services, Institute of Museum and Library Services

NOTES

1. "Convergence, n." OED Online. June 2018. Oxford University Press (accessed September 02, 2018).
2. W. Boyd Rayward, "Electronic Information and the Functional Integration of Libraries, Museums, and Archives" in Edward Higgs, ed., *History and Electronic Artefacts* (Oxford: Clarendon Press, 1998): 207–26. http://hdl.handle.net/2142/9474.
3. Emily Anne Proskine, "Google's Technicolor Dreamcoat: A Copyright Analysis of the Google Book Search Library Project," *Berkeley Technology Law Journal* 21 (2006): 213–40.
4. Chris Anderson, "The Long Tail," *Wired* (October 1, 2004). https://www.wired.com/2004/10/tail/.

Preface

The best professional education blends theory with reflective practice. John Dewey (1859–1952), who introduced new methods for teaching children, was equally interested in instructing teachers. For him, education was social and interactive; theory was best learned by doing. The "doing" could take place in the classroom or outside. In Dewey's time, apprenticeships and laboratory research were two ways of integrating theory and practice. Students still do "apprenticeships"—today, internships, residencies, clerkships, and practicums—and in the classroom new pedagogies and technologies stimulate fresh ways of thinking.

Dewey was on our minds while we were designing the Cultural Heritage Informatics (CHI) program at Simmons University's School of Library and Information Science. We define CHI as a field that examines the nexus of information and computing technology in cultural heritage institutions. This intersection has led to a cross-disciplinary approach that supports the creation, use, and preservation of cultural heritage. We have long observed the impact of technological innovation, people's access to and use of information, and how they communicate with one another. Our aim in *Libraries, Archives, and Museums Today: Insights from the Field* is to look at CHI through the lens of actual experience, revealed in the case studies that we present here. Some of these studies examine how libraries, archives, and museums (LAMs) have used technology to improve access to information and to facilitate communication about their collections.

We considered a variety of ways for students to study LAMs and other cultural heritage institutions and organizations—inside and outside the classroom. We already had strong relationships with professionals in heritage institutions: some of them taught for Simmons as adjuncts and professors of practice and conducted research with us, some supervised internships, and some hired our graduates. Still others worked with us on the development of the CHI program. As we learned about new practices and challenges in institutions, we decided to create case studies to document the many changes that are now taking place. We decided that the cases would be created by students and faculty individually and by students and faculty together. Of course, we could not have created the studies without the participation of our professional colleagues. Thus, the resulting cases blend our collective insights and perspectives. We decided to publish these case studies as a book so that others may learn as much as we have from them.

Another motivation for writing this book is that there are few sources for learning how libraries, archives, museums, and other cultural institutions are integrating new technologies, collaborating with one another, and finding new ways to engage with their users and audiences. One notable example of an initiative to study collaboration is OCLC's *Silos of the LAMs*,[1] a report published in 2008 in which five institutions participated in a series of workshops to explore collaborative and outcome-oriented projects. (One of the institutions that participated in the OCLC project is studied here: the Victoria and Albert Museum.) In rereading the report, we noted how much has changed in the past decade. For example, the report identifies a number of catalysts for change, which presumably make collaborations possible. Our case studies show that some of them, such as "incentives," "mooring," and "resources," no longer seem as important as when that report came out ten years ago. This signals the rapid change that evolving attitudes and technologies have made possible—even inevitable. Our observations of many additional institutions not included here reinforce this conclusion. Three catalysts that still seem relevant are "vision," "flexibility," and "trust." In other words, today collaboration seems to be much more common than is acknowledged.

Journals, as well as newsletters and reports issued by such organizations as the Association of Research Libraries, the Council of Library and Information Resources, and OCLC, also provide examples of individual or small collaborative projects, but no one source highlights projects and activities in the variety of institutions represented by the cases in this book. We hope our work will inspire additional case studies.

This book is designed for students, librarians, archivists, museum professionals, and others who work in cultural heritage settings. In the classroom, cases can be used in a variety of ways. Students can analyze them in group discussions or write responses or reflections. Cases can also be compared. For example, what traits are shared by institutions that collaborate, or innovate, or succeed with few resources?

Professionals can use this book to find out about current trends in heritage institutions. They can also learn how to deploy resources for strategic initiatives. We studied a wide variety of institutions, and there is much to be discovered in the various ways they have achieved their goals—or worked toward that achievement.

The fourteen cases presented here illustrate the many ways institutions have used new technologies to provide innovative programs and services to their users. In some, institutions have reconsidered, and occasionally refocused, their core missions. In others, institutions have reorganized their operations and services. Some of the case studies demonstrate innovation—sometimes with constrained resources—while others show what can happen when resources are too constrained. The studies also reveal that LAMs are often housed inside larger institutions whose top administrators do not always understand their missions, needs, and operations. Being part of a larger institution can be harmful to a library's mission. For example, several museum libraries have closed in recent years.[2] One of the things a reader of these studies can learn from them is how to deal with such a situation—and that "dealing with" administrators is not always the best way for LAMs to fulfill their responsibilities or reach their goals.

ORGANIZATION

We have divided the book into five sections:

Part I Digital Strategies

Part II Collaboration within and across Institutions

Part III Strategic Use of Resources

Part IV Institutions in Transition

Part V Culturally Sensitive Materials

In part I, the case studies examine an independent research library; a complex hybrid institution with historic buildings, libraries, archives, museum objects, and a publishing arm; a community-based archive; and a statewide network. Each institution or organization has managed complex digital projects, and two have depended on volunteers. The American Antiquarian Society has successfully deployed resources for its digital asset management program. The History Project in Boston, a community-based archive, is using digital initiatives to increase access to LGBT history—using volunteers. Historic New England's digitization activities are well integrated with its mission and strategic planning process. The Maine Memory Network exemplifies how a number of small institutions working together can build an effective statewide program to provide digital access to collections.

Part II illustrates various kinds of intra- and interinstitutional collaborations. Cases include a university, a museum, a public library, and a collaboration among public broadcasting stations and the Library of Congress. The American Archive of Public Broadcasting is a successful collaboration among public television stations and the Library of Congress. Cornell University has found ways to successfully collaborate across its libraries, IT, and other units of the university, and for some twenty years it has been a digital innovator. New York City's Museum of Modern Art is an example of successful collaboration across libraries, archives, curatorial departments, the museum store, and other units in the museum. The Boston Public Library provides digital services to its patrons and coordinates the statewide Digital Commonwealth Repository. A large public and research library, it has found ways to address the needs of its diverse audiences.

In part III, two institutions—the National Library of Australia (NLA) and the Victoria and Albert Museum—provide striking examples of the use of strategic resources to fund and sustain new programs. At the NLA, digital assets have been a driver for change since the mid-1990s. The Victoria and Albert Museum has coupled attention to collections management with the use of the web to refresh its image.

Part IV documents three institutions in transition. In the first case, an anonymous museum chose to move in a new direction and closed down its library without any staff input. The second institution, the American Textile History Museum, was forced to close. Its staff focused on finding the best homes for its extensive holdings and managed to transfer its collections to over one hundred institutions. The Peabody Essex Museum had planned to renovate the historic buildings that housed its library. Instead, it moved the collections several towns away. This case study looks at the distinguished history of the library and community reactions to the move.

Part V considers culturally sensitive materials and includes only one case, the Harvard Peabody Museum of Archaeology and Ethnology, though we predict that as institutions continue to expand their digitization projects, additional culturally sensitive materials will come to light. While we know anecdotally of how some institutions have handled such materials, further development of cases from which we can learn would be useful. This area would greatly benefit from a publication of best practices.

Appendix A provides the list of questions we used for our interviews, which structured our conversations and ultimately ranged over other topics as well; appendix B lists the people who were interviewed. The bibliography not only indicates our sources but should also serve as a guide for further reading on a broad spectrum of resources.

Libraries, Archives, and Museums Today reflects the practices of a variety of cultural heritage institutions and organizations, most of which operate in complex and constantly changing environments. This collection of cases will provide readers with a fresh understanding and appreciation of what makes many cultural institutions successful.

NOTES

1. Diane Zorich, Gunter Waibel, and Ricky Erway, *Beyond the Silos of the LAMs: Collaboration among Libraries, Archives and Museums* (Dublin, OH: OCLC, 2008), accessed July 21, 2018, www.oclc.org/research/publications/library/2008/2008-05.pdf.

2. See Art Libraries Society of North America (ARLIS), "State of Art Museum Libraries 2016," ARLIS/NA Museum Division White Paper, ARLIS, accessed July 28, 2018, https://www.arlisna.org/images/researchreports/State_of_Art_Museum_Libraries_2016.pdf. This publication provides an excellent overview of challenges facing art museum libraries today. ARLIS estimates that of the estimated 3,241 art museums in the United States, approximately two hundred have staffed libraries (p. 4).

Acknowledgments

We would like to thank the people who wrote or co-wrote the case studies in this volume: Emeline Dehn-Reynolds (Maine Memory Network), Brett Freiburger (Historic New England), Ross Harvey and Jaye Weatherburn (National Library of Australia), Bryce Roe and Lily Troia (American Archive of Public Broadcasting), and Samantha Strain (The History Project).

Thanks to the many people we interviewed, some of whom chose to be anonymous. Their insights were invaluable to the case studies and our teaching.

We thank Joyce Ray, a longtime colleague, for writing the foreword.

At Rowman & Littlefield, we thank Charles Harmon, an incomparable editor. He was immediately supportive of our idea to create a LAMs case-study book. Sandy Wood, now a freelance editor, added her superlative editorial touch.

A special thanks to the many students who have inspired us at the University of Arizona, the University of California, Los Angeles, and Simmons University. We owe a special debt to our Simmons students in LIS 477, "Digital Asset Management for Libraries, Archives, and Museums," and LIS 432, "Concepts in Cultural Heritage Informatics," who either wrote or critiqued case studies.

Two research assistants, Joel DeMelo and Eliana Fenyes, worked on various aspects of the book. Thanks are due to them for their hard work and patience.

Simmons awarded Peter Botticelli a grant from the Emily Hollowell Research Fund, which made it possible for him to travel to several sites. We also thank the Institute of Museum and Library Services for awarding us the grant "Curriculum, Cooperation, Convergence, Capacity: Four Cs for the Development of Cultural Heritage Institutions: Libraries, Museums, and

Archives in the Twenty-First Century," 2009–2012. Among the many benefits of their support was partnering with a number of LAMs, some of which are profiled in these cases.

Finally, we thank our partners, Judy Bygate, Manley Tuttle, and Sidney Berger.

Introduction

This book is about libraries, archives, and museums (LAMs) as they strive to meet the new challenges of the digital age while maintaining their historic role as repositories of material culture. Our mission as educators is to prepare information professionals for careers in institutional environments that are marked by great uncertainty and great promise. Our students clearly see the enduring value of books, records, and material objects as well as their digital equivalents, and they would like us to provide simple formulas for preserving and sharing information in the hybrid material-and-digital world in which we live today. But alas, there are no exact formulas. As educators, we have spent the last two decades—since the rise of the web in the mid-1990s—tracking efforts by LAMs to understand and utilize digital technology and, more importantly, to keep up with the rapid changes we have seen in user needs and expectations. It makes for a complicated story, especially given the remarkable diversity of collections, methods, and organizations we find in this sector. In a twist on Leo Tolstoy's famous observation that "happy families are alike; every unhappy family is unhappy in its own way," our experience in teaching suggests the opposite for LAMS—that they often fail for similar reasons (e.g., a lack of funding or poor leadership), while they tend to succeed by building unique collections and serving distinct audiences. With this book, we aim to help students and working professionals in the LAM sector understand and solve the challenges we face locally and as related professional disciplines.

Fortunately, it is not difficult to find common themes in the LAM story, and so here we attempt to show how recent experiences may be forming a new chapter in the five-thousand-year history of LAM repositories. From the scant evidence we have about the Ptolemaic Alexandrian Library (third century BC to its final destruction in around AD 642), scholars have concluded that it contained elements of libraries, archives, and museums and may have been a sort of proto-research institute as well, paving the way for the rich variety of cultural heritage institutions that have evolved over the past two millennia.[1] Ultimately, LAMs are united as a sector by the fundamental act of collecting, preserving, and facilitating access to things, be they books, archival records, and museum objects, as well as their digital equivalents today.

From our vantage point on the East Coast, we are often reminded of the role played by subscription libraries and athenaeums, which date back to the eighteenth century, before the establishment of public libraries and museums.[2] They were often conceived as hybrid institutions containing books, archives, art, and natural history collections. They were also designed as social institutions, featuring regular exhibitions and lecture series. For the Boston Athenaeum, it was a subject of debate in the mid-1800s whether the institution should focus principally on books or on art.[3] Books ultimately won out, and some of the Athenaeum's art collection was transferred or lent to Boston's Museum of Fine Arts after it opened in 1876. Similarly, after opening to the public in 1854, the Boston Public Library amassed books (its original sixteen thousand volume collection has expanded to roughly twenty million today) and a substantial art collection, including over one hundred thousand prints, giving patrons access to rich visual resources along with reading material.[4]

By the end of the nineteenth century, libraries, archives, and museums had begun to evolve distinct identities and methods; yet libraries continued to amass art collections, while museums continued to build library and archival collections. In other words, the hybrid nature of cultural institutions in the nineteenth century never went away, even with twentieth-century efforts to professionalize the LAM sector by dividing it into three disciplines, with the result that students now have a choice of graduate programs in library and information science, archives and records management, and museum studies. Each discipline has a solid academic foundation, and yet we find that Simmons University students (and those at similar schools) often find it confusing that a "library" degree (accredited by the American Library Association) can have an "archives" concentration attached to it. We have found many of our library/archives students pursuing internships and jobs in museums. Further muddying the disciplinary waters is the fact that museum studies programs may be tied to a variety of academic disciplines, including art history and anthropology.

Given the historical development of LAMs, it makes sense that with the rise of the web beginning in the 1990s, we've seen renewed efforts to promote collaboration across the disciplines, especially as institutions have turned their attention to digital collecting and the practical issues LAMs face in providing online access to collections. The practical challenges arising from digital technology may be vastly different from the issues faced by institutions such as the Boston Athenaeum and the Boston Public Library in the 1800s, and yet the overarching goal has remained the same—namely, providing an active cultural space and low-cost access to high-quality information resources. With the great potential of the web to reshape and enhance the historic mission of LAMs, it was significant that in the United States a merger occurred in 1996 between two federal agencies: the Library Programs Office of the Department of Education and the Institute of Museum Services. The new agency, the Institute of Museum and Library Services (IMLS), was created through legislation stipulating that the director serve a four-year term and that the leadership of the agency alternate between library and museum professionals. The mission of IMLS is to "advance, support, and empower America's museums, libraries, and related organizations through grant-making, research, and policy development."[5] Over the past two decades, IMLS has awarded hundreds of grants to promote innovation and particularly to foster greater collaboration among LAMs. Comparable investments have been made in the European Union, Australia, Canada, and many other countries as well. In many cases, technology has served as the focus for grants, whether for digitization projects intended to widen access to material collection objects or for efforts to build the capacity LAMs need to acquire and preserve born-digital objects at scale.

By the mid-2000s, IMLS was actively working to advance the conversation around technology, in part by funding LAM graduate programs to develop new curricula around the broad theme of "digital curation."[6] This term may be defined as a whole life-cycle approach to managing digital assets, encompassing the full set of activities from the creation of digital assets to online access and long-term preservation. It promotes an explicitly interdisciplinary perspective for LAMs, moving away from the relatively specialized "silos" that characterize paper-based libraries and archives, as well as museums grounded in curating material objects. We can directly link digital curation to the long-standing idea of convergence, which highlights the commonalities rather than the differences between LAMs—an idea that has taken on new currency with the rise of online access systems that enable users to search for and use information resources with minimal regard for the twentieth-century silos into which LAMs have often sorted material collections.

To bring the LAM sector closer together, IMLS has hosted conferences, including the landmark Cultural Heritage Information Professionals (CHIPS) Workshop held in 2008. CHIPS brought together an eclectic group of LAM professionals and educators (including the authors of this book) representing over thirty institutions. An explicit goal was to find points of convergence, with the larger aim of envisioning a new role for "cultural heritage information professionals" beyond librarian, archivist, or museum professional. The conference organizers and participants envisioned a more explicitly interdisciplinary perspective in LAM education. It was assumed that LAMs would maintain their historic mission as repositories of material objects, but at the same time the rise of online access was clearly leading users to view LAM collections as information resources that are, or should be, interoperable and accessible via standard methods and systems. With digital resources expected to grow dramatically in value for users, it followed that LAM professionals would need to be educated in new ways to address "the changing nature of information work in libraries, archives, and museums"[7] as online access systems continued to reshape user needs and expectations, leading potentially to a convergence in the LAM sector—or, perhaps, a kind of reconvergence that might rekindle the enterprising spirit of the nineteenth-century athenaeums for the digital age.

As we observe the world of LAMs on our students' behalf, we find ourselves continually assessing the sector's progress and seeking to identify change factors, both technological and organizational, that might prove decisive in our students' career paths. We began this book with the big question of what the LAM sector has been able to accomplish over the first two decades of the digital age and what key challenges LAMs are facing now. In particular, we wanted to know whether interdisciplinary collaboration, as envisioned by IMLS since the 1990s, has made a genuine impact in helping institutions better use technology in engaging audiences. In seeking answers to these questions, we have taken an empirical approach, with much of our data coming from semistructured interviews with LAM professionals. Appendix A includes the basic set of questions we asked each institution; in general, we sought to examine how they have adapted their workflows and organizational structures to take full advantage of digital technology. In theoretical terms, we have aimed, on the one hand, to respect and represent the vast diversity of LAM collections and institutional histories and, on the other hand, to look for patterns or common themes in the experiences of individual practitioners and LAM institutions. This naturally led us to adopt as our basic methodological approach the case study, helpfully defined by Robert Yin as "an empirical method that investigates a contemporary phenomenon (the 'case') in depth and within its real-world context, especially when the boundaries between phenomenon and context may not be clearly evident."[8] In other words, case studies provide a way to capture varied and complex narratives without forcing individual cases into generalizable categories. Therefore, our selection of cases is not meant to be representative of the LAM field as a whole. Rather, it is meant to be exploratory—to act as a starting point to which more cases might be added and that leaves room for updates to reflect future developments. By limiting our theoretical claims for the cases, we have also adopted the normative goal of identifying successful as well as unsuccessful instances of collaboration and institutional adaptation. Our larger hope is that by examining a rich and varied sampling of institutions, we might identify factors that make for successful cross-disciplinary collaborations, as well as common impediments that may limit or derail collaboration.

In developing case studies for this book, we aimed to give working practitioners a realistic and practical view of how the work of LAMs has been changing in recent years. The cases presented here reflect our ongoing work at Simmons to establish a new, explicitly interdisciplinary approach to graduate education for LAM professionals as embodied in the master's concentration we launched in 2015 as Cultural Heritage Informatics (CHI). This still-evolving curriculum is part of a larger movement in which graduate schools featuring library and information science, archival studies, and museum studies have created new degree programs or concentrations designed to teach LAM professionals the advanced technical and organizational skills needed for hands-on work with digital information. A common aim of these programs, including CHI, has been to avoid or prevent the intellectual siloing of information professionals, even with the realization that many of our graduates will end up specializing in particular branches of the extended LAM family. We hope that those students who take the core CHI courses will become reflective professionals with minds open to the wide range of methods and tools currently available to manage and preserve cultural heritage as it appears in the LAM sector as a whole. For us, the development of the CHI program began in earnest with a 2009 IMLS grant,[9] which helped us to understand how case studies and field experiences by students can provide rich insights into the complex environments in which LAM professionals are working today. Above all, our experience in developing and teaching students in CHI has highlighted for us the current dynamism of the LAM sector and the need to observe carefully, and with a critical eye, the choices being made by institutions as they learn more about user needs in the digital age.

In selecting cases to include in this book, we considered a wide range of libraries, archives, and museums, as well as hybrid institutions such as Historic New England, which includes historic properties along with books, manuscripts, archives, and museum objects. We started with a list of roughly thirty institutions. While we tried to focus on what we regard as success stories, we have also included a few cases that represent institutional failures of one kind or another, such as one anonymized case about a museum that decided to close its library despite a recent and successful capital campaign. We also chose to include the American Textile History Museum, which recently closed and dispersed its collection. Through subsequent research, we narrowed down the list to the institutions included here, which are grouped around a set of five overarching themes that structure the book. Part I focuses on relatively small institutions seeking to innovate with limited technology resources. By contrast, part II examines larger institutions for which collaboration across institutional boundaries is a possible means to pool local resources and build the digital infrastructure needed to scale up online resources. Likewise, part III focuses on strategies employed by two large institutions that have been successful innovators in recent years. In part IV, we examine LAMs that have failed or that have made deliberate cuts to resources for certain collections or services; we label these as institutions in transition or facing uncertain outcomes for key strategic decisions. Finally, in part V we examine an area of emerging concern for the LAM sector: the treatment of culturally sensitive materials, especially as they are made more accessible online.

NOTES

1. Kim Ryholt, "Libraries in Ancient Egypt," in *Ancient Libraries*, ed. Jason König, Katerina Oikonomopoulou, and Greg Woolf (Cambridge: Cambridge University Press, 2013), 23–27.
2. Prominent among these institutions in New England are the Boston Athenaeum, founded in 1807, and the Providence Athenaeum, which dates back to 1836. In Pennsylvania, the Athenaeum of Philadelphia was founded in 1814.
3. Hina Hirayama, *"With Eclat": The Boston Athenaeum and the Origin of the Museum of Fine Arts* (Boston: Boston Athenaeum, 2013).
4. Martha R. Mahard, "An Unparalleled Opportunity: Creating an Inventory of the Print Collection at the Boston Public Library," *Art Documentation* 37, no. 1 (spring 2018).
5. Institute of Museum and Library Services, accessed July 16, 2018, https://www.imls.gov.
6. Joyce Ray, "The Rise of Digital Curation and Cyberinfrastructure: From Experimentation to Implementation and Maybe Integration," *Library Hi Tech* 30, no. 4 (2012): 604–22.
7. Cultural Heritage Information Professionals (CHIPS) Workshop Report (2008), p. 3. The final report was written by Paul Marty of Florida State University. Source: marty.cci.fsu.edu.
8. Robert K. Yin, *Case Study Research and Applications: Design and Methods*, 6th ed. (Thousand Oaks, CA: Sage, 2018), 15.
9. The grant was titled "Curriculum, Cooperation, Convergence, Capacity: Four Cs for the Development of Cultural Heritage Institutions" and ran 2009–2012.

Part I

Digital Strategies

Chapter One

The American Antiquarian Society

Digital Asset Management in an Independent Research Library

Peter Botticelli

RESEARCH LIBRARIES AND DIGITIZATION

In recent years, digitization projects by research libraries[1] have resulted in large numbers of digital surrogates representing significant portions of their permanent collections. Consequently, we can now begin to observe the wider impact of digitization on the workflows, technology infrastructure, and online presence of research libraries and their collections. Here we present a case study showing how one institution, the American Antiquarian Society (AAS), has been adapting to the demands of creating and managing "digital assets," a term we use broadly to refer to all forms of collection documentation, along with digital images, acting as surrogates for material collection objects. Like many other research libraries today, AAS has moved beyond the early, experimental stages of digitization and is now committed to expanding access to digital assets in line with the growing expectations of online users. Judging by the quality of data provided to us, we believe the case of AAS offers useful insights into how digitization has been progressively reshaping library services, particularly the staff workflows and technologies needed to manage digital assets. The recent experience of AAS also highlights the practical issues and uncertainties libraries face as they seek to define best practices for managing digital assets.

As we explored these issues, the data generously provided by AAS enabled us to draw a detailed picture showing how a two-hundred-year-old research library has gone about building and adapting its digital infrastructure and services to meet user needs in a rapidly changing technology environment. In a wider context we found that, as a case study, the experience of AAS offers a useful way to test and refine the "digital library" concept, which has been an active area of research since the 1990s and has influenced the development of technologies designed for managing digital assets in libraries, including Fedora.[2] Concurrently with the rise of the web, digital libraries have been envisioned as network-based computing infrastructures, often consisting of a flexible bundle of tools or services tailored as much to humans as to machines. Treating the digital library as a network as opposed to a self-contained entity, Christine Borgman, for one, emphasizes the social dimension of the library as a locus for information that is "constructed, collected, and organized by (and for) a community of users, and their functional capabilities support the information needs and uses of that community."[3]

The design and composition of a digital library, as a sociotechnical system, was expected to vary substantially depending on local user needs and available technologies. In fact, by the mid-2000s, libraries, archives, and museums (LAMs) had a range of systems from which to choose for managing and providing access to the digital surrogates they were beginning to amass through digitization projects, and many institutions were in the early stages of planning digital "repositories"—a broader term covering the use of digital library technologies by all types of LAMs—to support a variety of workflows and institutional objectives, such as open access to scholarly works[4] and data sharing within and across research disciplines.[5] In this context, our goal in studying AAS was to understand how digital repositories have evolved since they first began to emerge in the early 2000s. In particular, we aimed to explore the organizational and technical challenges research libraries have faced in building and maintaining digital repositories. As we will see, the experience of AAS suggests that research libraries have found creative and effective ways to manage digital assets despite resource constraints and a historically rapid rate of technology obsolescence.

INTERVIEWS

Our data gathering at AAS centered on two rounds of semistructured interviews, with an initial round in spring 2015 and a follow-up round in spring 2016. Both rounds included a group interview with the following senior AAS staff members: Ellen Dunlap, president; Thomas Knoles, Marcus A. McCorison Librarian; Nick Conti, director of information technology; Lauren Hewes, Andrew W. Mellon Curator of Graphic Arts; and Molly O'Hagan Hardy, digital humanities curator. In addition we conducted individual interviews with the above staff members, plus Kayla Haveles Hopper, outreach coordinator. We were also given access to a number of internal documents with details on AAS's digital workflows and a history of digital repository planning efforts.

Our interview questions focused on the current technologies and workflows in use by AAS to create and manage digital assets. We asked what tools and systems are currently in use, how they function in practice, and about plans to change or add to AAS's existing infrastructure. However, from early on, the interviews provided a rich seam of historical data as well as information about current practices for creating and managing digital assets. We found AAS staff remarkably open to discussing the history of digital projects at AAS, which led us to uncover a number of important turning points that led to the adoption of new technologies in response both to changes in internal as well as external user needs and to situations in which existing technologies had or were about to become obsolete. With this data, the case study naturally evolved from a static view of existing technologies and methods for managing digital assets into a more detailed examination of the process whereby AAS has constructed a digital repository in recent years, in keeping with AAS's institutional mission and adapting to changes in the wider technology landscape.

HISTORY OF AAS

Founded in 1812, AAS has a collecting policy that focuses on documenting the print culture of the United States, Canada, and the West Indies through 1876. With a collection of roughly four million items, AAS is a leading repository for early American books, including two-thirds of all known American books published before the 1820s, plus extensive holdings of newspapers, sheet music, and a wide range of graphic arts materials. Despite its dedication to material culture, AAS has a history of adopting new technologies to widen access to its collections, starting with microprint projects in the 1950s with a commercial partner, Readex. By the mid-2000s, AAS was actively pursuing digital licensing agreements, in which publishers were granted exclusive online distribution rights for fixed periods in exchange for funding the creation of digital surrogates, with AAS retaining full control of digital images once the agreement expired.[6]

At the same time, AAS actively pursued in-house digitization efforts, including a 2004 project that resulted in digital surrogates for a set of five thousand lithographs, which were managed with a newly created Microsoft Access database. A critical project in this period involved digitizing roughly sixteen thousand records in the Mathew Carey Papers, an important collection of the business records and correspondence of an influential publisher who immigrated to Philadelphia from Ireland in the 1780s.[7] After acquiring this collection in the late 1920s, AAS created a much-used index of over six thousand names that appear in the Mathew Carey records; this resource was an obvious choice to digitize and make accessible as a database, with digital images of the records themselves.[8] Initially, the digital images were distributed on DVDs, but it was clear to AAS that a robust online access system was needed for this and other digitized resources.

By the late 2000s AAS had come to view in-house digital projects as a critical factor in raising the visibility of its graphic arts and manuscripts collections, which had tended to receive less public exposure in the past than its larger and more comprehensive collections of books and newspapers, which publishers had often favored for distribution through microform and later via online databases. To rectify this imbalance, AAS's curator of graphic arts, Gigi Barnhill, became a strong advocate for in-house digitization projects and for building a locally hosted digital repository that could display images effectively within AAS's own web domain, with direct links to item-level catalog records. Upon Barnhill's retirement in 2010, Lauren Hewes became curator of graphic arts (after serving as assistant curator beginning in 2005), and she too was no less determined to see AAS host a digital repository representing the graphic arts collection, while Thomas Knoles, as librarian and curator of manuscripts, had a similar view from the perspective of the AAS manuscripts collection.

BUILDING A DIGITAL REPOSITORY

An important step forward came in 2009, when AAS received a two-year grant from the National Endowment for the Humanities for a major digitization project titled "Prints in the Parlor," which aimed to digitize a selection of engravings representing images that would have commonly appeared in American households from roughly the 1820s to the 1870s.[9] This grant enabled AAS to scale up its in-house digitization capabilities, to hire a full-time photographer (previously a part-time position), and to reallocate some catalogers' time to creating descriptive metadata for digital surrogates. In general, by the time of the "Prints in the Parlor" project, AAS had established mature, routine workflows for creating digital assets. But the library was still in the early stages of building an online repository to manage and provide access to its newly created digital assets. Thus, as the grant got underway in 2009, AAS formed a Digital Assets Planning Group, following a number of earlier planning efforts, with the aim of studying the numerous options then available for digital repository systems. The planning group included Nick Conti, director of information technology; Christine Graham-Ward, visual materials cataloger; Lauren Hewes, curator of graphic arts; Thomas Knoles, librarian and curator of manuscripts; and Jaclyn Penny, image rights and design librarian. The group recognized an immediate need to replace the Access database (what AAS called its image management system, or IMS) it had been using, as this system had already exceeded its capacity before "Prints in the Parlor." From the planning group's perspective, AAS's immediate need was to provide effective access to a growing body of digital surrogates, although the preservation of digital assets was also recognized as a long-term need. Ultimately, the planning group decided to shut down the IMS and to replace it with a new system, nicknamed GIGI—standing for "graphical interface of gathered images" but also in honor of Gigi Barnhill—which went live in 2012, as the "Prints in the Parlor" grant was concluding.

In evaluating digital repository systems, the planning group had a few basic criteria. First, it had to have metadata support, especially the capacity to import and update catalog metadata into the repository, as AAS sought to limit the need to create metadata specifically for the online repository. At the same time, AAS needed a system that could handle a range of metadata schemas, from full MARC records to minimal descriptive records created for noncollection items such as library event photographs. Second, AAS needed a repository system that could be installed and maintained at relatively low cost, a factor that ultimately favored proprietary applications, despite the desire of AAS staff members to support the development of open source technologies in libraries. Also, due to the relatively small scale of AAS's digital holdings at the time, the planning group ruled out third-party (or "cloud") storage solutions in favor of using local servers to host the repository. Third, AAS needed a system that could easily support varying levels of user access. As the repository was envisioned, internal staff users would have access to all images at all resolutions. In turn, public users would be able to view selected images, usually at a medium resolution, while licensees would be given access to selected images at a high resolution.

In assessing AAS's choice of repository systems, it is important to consider how GIGI needed to be fit into the relatively complex digital infrastructure AAS had already built over time. This included an integrated library system (ILS) for the catalog, plus a separate application for access services, which was used to track collection objects and to fulfill requests from patrons and staff. AAS also had an access system, nicknamed Clarence, for its extensive newspaper metadata. Internally, the conservation department used an Access database to manage its workflow, with conservation treatments also documented in the catalog. Thus, well before GIGI went online in 2012, virtually all AAS staff were already creating many types of valuable digital assets, using specialized tools and workflows tailored to their particular needs. Consequently, for GIGI to replace existing systems, it would need to be both powerful and highly flexible in its capabilities, supporting internal users no less well than external users.

In reality the Digital Assets Planning Group did not expect GIGI to become an all-purpose digital repository, especially as they were not able to identify any applications that met all their needs in full. Rather, the group viewed GIGI as a necessary extension to the functionality of systems already in use at AAS, particularly the ILS. A key objective for GIGI was to be able to link digital images directly to the MARC catalog records, reflecting the institution's strong commitment to item-level cataloging for all its digitized items. For this reason, the group considered the option of using a plugin application that would enable the ILS to display images within the OPAC. When this option proved too costly and technically impractical, the group decided that GIGI would require a stand-alone system.

In deciding which repository system to adopt, the planning group focused on a small number of applications in widespread use by libraries and museums, including some that had originated in the commercial market for digital asset management (DAM) solutions, which tended to focus on the needs of private firms that produce and maintain large quantities of digital content, including in the advertising and media sectors. Ultimately, AAS chose Extensis Portfolio, a proprietary DAM system that was in widespread use by photographers; AAS was aware of at least two major museums that had adopted it to manage their image collections. The planning group appreciated the fact that as an image-centered repository system, Portfolio supported multiple file formats and was able to deliver high-resolution images as well as compressed, yet still relatively large, JPEG images created on the fly, thereby saving storage space. AAS also welcomed the fact that Portfolio supported rich, MARC-level metadata as well as minimalist approaches, such as Dublin Core, and included the capacity to import existing metadata in batches from other systems, including the ILS.

ONLINE DISCOVERY AND ACCESS TO DIGITAL SURROGATES

Since it was launched in 2012, GIGI has proven effective for managing AAS's growing body of digital surrogates and for providing access to internal as well as external users. In effect, the effort to build a permanent digital repository has remained a work in progress and continues to be a source of active discussion and planning within AAS. In practical terms, AAS has found a number of important limitations with the Portfolio software, as indicated below. For one thing, as noted above, the Digital Assets Planning Group envisioned GIGI as a tool for managing and providing access to digital surrogates and not as an alternative to the catalog for discovery purposes. The hope was that GIGI itself would simply import whatever metadata was needed directly from existing catalog records. However, Nick Conti found the process of importing catalog metadata into GIGI more difficult than expected due to software compatibility issues between the ILS and Portfolio. Moreover, the decision to install a public-facing repository system independent of the ILS reinforced the need to create metadata tailored to GIGI. For instance, AAS owns a collection of fifty-four photographs of the Tuskegee Institute, which are cataloged in MARC at the collection level.[10] This provides a useful entry point to this relatively small collection, but because the items can be viewed individually in GIGI, AAS found it necessary to add some item-level description to each image as it appears in Portfolio.

As graphic arts curator, Lauren Hewes was concerned that if GIGI relied exclusively on catalog records, users might become confused as they discovered objects cataloged through collection-level "inventory" records rather than as individual items. For instance, AAS has a catalog record for a collection of sixty paper ream wrappers[11] with digital surrogates available in GIGI; the catalog record is linked to a canned search in GIGI, which retrieves the images using the catalog record number (505205) for the collection, which is also used to label each image. Within GIGI itself, AAS has tagged each image with the keyword "Ream Wrappers," giving the user a practical way to search for these images; otherwise it would be necessary to know the exact catalog number for the collection or to search the catalog first. While GIGI actually provides very sparse metadata for this collection, creating records in GIGI does require a workflow and some staff time—a trade-off Hewes believes is necessary to allow for consistent retrieval at the item level.

Actually, the decision to add some metadata to GIGI has had a significant, and unexpected, impact on AAS's overall web presence simply because GIGI is open to indexing by search engines while the ILS is not. Google searches have led to a significant increase in AAS's web traffic, along with more requests for licensed images. While welcome, this higher web profile has also raised a dilemma insofar as GIGI has to compete for cataloging resources while representing a small fraction of AAS's total collection. From AAS's perspective, the catalog remains the logical starting point for discovery, especially as it provides direct links to GIGI as well as to third-party databases maintained by AAS's commercial partners.

While AAS has clearly benefitted from having search engines index GIGI, the repository itself has a decidedly minimalist interface that works best displaying one image at a time, with limited options for representing groups of images and for helping users navigate through the pages of a book or manuscript. This was more of a problem for manuscripts than for the graphic arts collection, which contains many prints and photographs that may be viewed appropriately in isolation. Nick Conti was able to customize GIGI to enable users to click through a set of images, but it remained a priority to find more appealing ways to display complex digital objects. In fact, by June 2016, GIGI included over seventy thousand total page scans of manuscripts representing 156 different collections and roughly eighteen thousand page scans of books, as opposed to thirty-eight thousand images representing the graphic arts collection (including prints, drawings, and photographs) and just under four thousand scans of miscellaneous collection objects.

Besides the need to display images in a logical sequence, GIGI has also highlighted the need to support visual browsing of surrogate images. As AAS outreach coordinator, Kayla Hopper has found GIGI to be a valuable, if sometimes frustrating, resource for educational programs and publications such as brochures, annual reports, and the AAS blog, all of which make extensive use of digital images. For example, in searching for relevant images of Abraham Lincoln, Hopper might begin with a simple keyword search in GIGI, then browse the resulting thumbnail images to find those suitable for use by teachers or in an AAS publication. In general, from an outreach perspective, Hopper sees visual browsing as a potent way to engage audiences beyond academic researchers, who have long been the library's core group of patrons and for whom the catalog is likely to remain the default tool for discovery. However, with the current limitations of GIGI's interface, Hopper has often been forced to rely on images she already knows are in GIGI or that have been recommended to her by the AAS photographer or other staff members. Also, in sharing images, Hopper and other staff members have found it necessary to use canned searches—involving long, unintuitive URLs—because Portfolio does not support the creation of permanent URLs for items in the repository. This is especially cumbersome in retrieving images of books or manuscripts, as a separate canned search is needed for each successive page.

ADOPTION OF OMEKA FOR EXHIBITS

Given the demand for better visual browsing of collections and the general desire to enrich its overall online presence, AAS began to implement a new open-source technology, Omeka, in 2014—just two years after launching GIGI. For AAS, a key consideration in adopting Omeka was its relative ease of use as a tool for exhibiting digital surrogates in a rich collection context, with metadata that is open to indexing by search engines and with graphical elements that can be easily customized for particular exhibitions. At the same time, however, AAS clearly viewed Omeka as a substitute for neither GIGI nor the ILS. Rather, it saw Omeka as an add-on to the institution's existing digital infrastructure, one that would enhance the visibility of AAS's collection and fit well with the existing skills and needs of AAS's staff. This view matches Borgman's theoretical concept of a digital repository as a complex and organic or evolving infrastructure, with technology components that are regularly adopted and rejected as human needs and the larger technology environment develop over time. Thus, AAS staff saw adopting Omeka as a tool to create online exhibitions and a way to build directly on the capabilities (and shortcomings) of GIGI and the ILS.

It's also worth noting that AAS's use of Omeka followed a number of earlier projects, going back to the early 2000s, when staff created online exhibitions using HTML pages published on the AAS website. This approach was effective in providing access to relatively small numbers of digitized collection items, including, for instance, the 150 ambrotypes[12] and 230 daguerreotypes[13] in the photograph collection or the roughly two hundred items in the European Political Print Collection,[14] which have been made accessible through linked HTML pages on the AAS website. These projects made a useful contribution to AAS's online presence yet required more time and a relatively high level of technological skill by comparison with Omeka, which has enabled AAS to produce exhibitions more quickly and with minimal technological support.

Thus far Molly O'Hagan Hardy, digital humanities curator, has undertaken much of the planning and research for AAS's Omeka-based exhibitions, beginning with the "Isaiah Thomas Broadside Ballads"[15] project, which grew out of a proposed book project that would have reproduced a bound collection of early American songs. AAS believed it would reach a larger audience online through a searchable, interactive exhibition with rich contextual information and formal item-level MARC records exported from the catalog. Since this initial project, AAS has completed roughly a half dozen exhibitions in Omeka, and at present up to nine staff members are using it actively. Omeka has given AAS staff a practical means to create exhibitions that provide a scholarly perspective on otherwise overlooked parts of the collection, going well beyond the basic access points found in the catalog. Thus, a recent Omeka exhibition describes ongoing scholarly efforts to preserve the Algonquian languages, making use of early American translations in the AAS collection.[16] Another exhibition, titled "Mill Girls in Nineteenth-Century Print," provides a historical context for digitized prints at AAS that depict the social conditions of women who worked in the New England textile industry in the 1800s.[17]

TECHNOLOGY OBSOLESCENCE

In just a few years since it was launched in 2012, GIGI has grown to include over one hundred thousand digital images and become an essential part of AAS's technology infrastructure by extending digital access to collections through the ILS, Omeka exhibitions, direct browsing of images, and web search engines. While Extensis Portfolio has been largely successful in meeting AAS's image management needs, by 2015 GIGI had reached a turning point. First, AAS reached the maximum storage capacity supported by the current version of Portfolio. In the near term, Conti was able to work around this problem by managing manuscript images as a separate collection, but GIGI was clearly already in need of a substantial upgrade or replacement to handle the institution's growing volume of digital assets. The obsolescence issues facing GIGI became more urgent after Extensis announced plans for a major redesign of Portfolio and to discontinue support for the older version. Consequently, by fall 2015 AAS faced a clear choice of whether to upgrade to the new version of Portfolio or to adopt a different system to support GIGI.

In planning GIGI's immediate and long-term future, AAS's decision-making process has been directly informed by the rapid obsolescence it experienced with Portfolio and by the ever-present need to minimize IT costs without sacrificing the functionality needed to manage a growing body of digital assets and to meet the rising expectations of internal as well as external users seeking access to them. On the whole, GIGI has led to a growing demand for digital images by external users as well as by internal users creating online exhibitions and a variety of AAS-related publications. In turn, the growing demand for images has raised the issue of whether AAS should retain a dedicated digital asset manager or distribute this responsibility across multiple units and staff positions. In fact, AAS has opted for the latter approach, and even with GIGI's continued growth, the institution remains committed to digital asset management as a shared responsibility.

That said, a number of AAS staff members have had to dedicate a substantial amount of time to the management of GIGI, taking time away from other collection-related activities. A particular issue has concerned the distribution of high-resolution images, both internally and externally, which requires manual intervention due to access restrictions on these assets. With Portfolio, staff have found management of GIGI access privileges time-consuming and the use of canned searches to point users to particular images cumbersome. As a work-around, they routinely copy image files from GIGI and deliver them to patrons or other staff through Dropbox, for which AAS has an institutional subscription. As a consequence, for high-resolution images at least, GIGI's role has essentially been reduced to one of storage more than access.

As he considered whether to upgrade or replace Portfolio as GIGI's infrastructure, Nick Conti was concerned that the new version of Portfolio might offer fewer options for customization than the previous version; in particular, he believed that a separate access system—using an API to transfer data from Portfolio—might be needed to meet AAS's access needs, a solution that would likely cost more to build and maintain than GIGI had using the old Portfolio. Also, in the years following the launch of GIGI, Conti had followed the advances made in open source tools for updating and migrating library metadata records in bulk, and he was keen to take advantage of such tools, especially as he had been forced to update metadata in relatively small batches with GIGI's existing technology.

In fact, the obsolescence of Portfolio gave AAS an opportunity to reconsider GIGI's entire role as an access system, especially given the costs involved in maintaining a system like Portfolio and, in particular, the need to create metadata specifically for digital surrogates appearing in GIGI, as opposed to using the already existing catalog records for items in the collection. One option for AAS was to limit direct public access to GIGI and instead to reemphasize the catalog as the main tool for discovery—with links to images stored in GIGI attached to catalog records as they appeared in the OPAC. This approach would limit the visibility of AAS collections in search engines but save resources by avoiding the need to supplement the catalog with metadata created exclusively for GIGI. Given the limitations of the ILS as a search interface, AAS was hopeful that ongoing efforts to develop next-generation access systems—including Fedora-based systems like Hydra—would eventually allow AAS and other libraries to expose their catalog metadata and digital surrogates more effectively at an affordable cost. AAS staff were also optimistic about the long-term potential of the Digital Public Library of America as a collaboration among libraries, with the aim of developing open source repository technologies and common approaches to sharing collections online.

By late 2015, AAS had decided that it would be necessary to replace Portfolio as the infrastructure behind GIGI. As Nick Conti and others considered alternative systems, they decided that open source repository systems, such as Hydra, had not yet progressed to the point of being cost-effective for AAS. At the same time, AAS was understandably skeptical of proprietary solutions, including the new version of Portfolio, which would stretch AAS's IT budget while potentially becoming obsolete in a few years' time, especially as open source technologies continued to improve. With these factors in mind, AAS decided that an interim solution was needed for GIGI, one that would complement the AAS's existing infrastructure, including the ILS and Omeka, and provide an inexpensive way to store and distribute digital surrogates for roughly the next three to five years, at which time GIGI might face obsolescence once again. Looking ahead, AAS staff were optimistic that the movement toward linked open data would prove transformative for libraries as they continued to digitize collections and further engage audiences online. For instance, AAS is currently digitizing the Printers' File, an extensive card catalog with biographical information on early American printers, which dates back to the 1920s and until recently existed only in paper form. Once the data on the cards is translated into a machine-readable format and organized in the proposed Database of the Early American Book Trades, the Printers' File will have great potential value as a linked open data resource for scholars.[18]

As a next step for GIGI, in spring 2016 Conti began developing what he named "SimpleDAM," which he envisioned as the simplest, least expensive solution to AAS's immediate needs for the GIGI repository. He was able to develop SimpleDAM quickly, using PHP code derived from a number of existing open source applications. SimpleDAM consists of a set of tools for managing and displaying images stored in directories on a local server, with no metadata attached to each image beyond a controlled ID number. This was a deliberate trade-off on Conti's part, as the decision to eliminate descriptive metadata from GIGI made it feasible to do without the functionality of a database application, thereby reducing GIGI's maintenance costs to an absolute minimum while retaining the ability of other systems, including the ILS, to link to images stored in GIGI. SimpleDAM also includes a basic interface that can display images up to four thousand pixels in size, and it enables users to navigate through sets of related images.

The design of SimpleDAM represents an important shift in AAS's approach to digital asset management as well as for GIGI itself, especially as the adoption of SimpleDAM is intended to limit users to the catalog for discovery, while making the contents of GIGI more or less invisible to search engines. Conti understood that both internal as well as external users of GIGI could find the ILS a more cumbersome way to search for and browse images. Yet he believed that AAS already had a potential way to solve this problem, through its growing use of Omeka to create digital exhibitions with rich contextual metadata that was exposed to search engines. Conti was hopeful that AAS would continue to create new Omeka exhibitions that would eventually represent large portions of the total collection. As an example, AAS might eventually host an Omeka exhibition for each of its manuscript collections, giving users a context-rich and visually appealing way to explore page images by each author.

CONCLUSION

The AAS case study deepens our understanding of how digital repositories have been shaped by social as well as technological factors in libraries. For AAS, the initial development of GIGI represented years of planning and experience with digital projects. The design of GIGI was also influenced by the particular technologies that were already in use at AAS and also by the existing market for repository applications in 2012, when GIGI was implemented. Once installed, GIGI came to play an important, if complicated, role in AAS's workflows, one that required substantial adjustments and workarounds by staff members. The rapid obsolescence of GIGI marked an important shift not just in the Portfolio application itself but also in the wider organizational context in which GIGI may be used by AAS staff as well as by external users. As AAS has developed and refined its workflows for creating and managing digital images, the institution has managed—despite resource limitations—to build up a complex digital infrastructure that includes multiple database applications supporting GIGI, the ILS, and other systems supporting access services and conservation functions.

In broader terms, AAS offers useful insights into how a major research library has gone about planning, building, and maintaining a digital repository—understood here as the complex and evolving set of tools and services needed to manage digital assets. The recent experience of AAS clearly shows how libraries have adopted a range of new technologies in response to changes in user needs. Our findings also show how the rapid rate of technology obsolescence in recent years has greatly complicated efforts by libraries to make technology plans and to create routine workflows. Nonetheless, AAS's recent experience suggests that while libraries are operating in a fast-changing technology environment, institutions can be effective in managing obsolescence risks and in meeting the needs of internal as well as external users. The case of AAS may offer practical guidance for libraries as they address the challenges involved in managing digital assets as they continue to accumulate through successive digitization projects. The experience of AAS also reinforces the need for case studies to reveal wider patterns in the library community regarding the adoption and obsolescence of repository systems, and it highlights the need to develop robust theoretical frameworks to help libraries plan their workflows and to anticipate changes in user needs as they continually revise and add components to their digital repositories.

NOTES

1. As a category, research libraries cover a broad range of institutions and collection policies. For our purposes here, we can simply point to the membership of the Independent Research Libraries Association (http://irla.lindahall.org), which includes the American Antiquarian Society.

2. Sandra Payette and Carl Lagoze, "Flexible and Extensible Digital Object and Repository Architecture (FEDORA)," in *Research and Advanced Technology for Digital Libraries: Second European Conference, ECDL '98 Heraklion, Crete, Greece, September 21–23, 1998 Proceedings*. Lecture Notes in Computer Science 1513 (Berlin: Springer, 1998), 41–59.

3. Christine Borgman, "What Are Digital Libraries? Competing Visions," *Information Processing and Management* 35, no. 3 (May 1999): 234. See also Rob Kling, "What Is Social Informatics and Why Does It Matter," *D-Lib Magazine* 5, no. 1 (January 1999), http://www.dlib.org/dlib/january99/kling/01kling.html.

4. Peter Suber, *Open Access* (Cambridge, MA: MIT Press, 2012).

5. Clifford Lynch, "Institutional Repositories: Essential Infrastructure for Scholarship in the Digital Age," *portal: Libraries and the Academy* 3, no. 2 (April 2003): 327–336.

6. Deanna Marcum, "Searching for Sustainability: Strategies from Eight Digitized Special Collections," Ithaka S+R, 2013, accessed July 24, 2018, http://sr.ithaka.org/wp-content/uploads/2015/08/SR_IMLS_20140129.pdf.

7. "Finding Aid for the Mathew Carey Papers, 1785–1859," American Antiquarian Society (AAS), accessed July 24, 2018, http://www.americanantiquarian.org/mathew-carey-papers-finding-aid.

8. "The Mathew Carey Papers, 1785–1859," AAS, accessed July 24, 2018, http://www.americanantiquarian.org/careydatabase.

9. Lauren Hewes, "Prints in the Parlor," *Past Is Present* (blog), April 2, 2010, accessed July 24, 2018, http://pastispresent.org/2010/good-sources/prints-in-the-parlor.

10. "General Catalog of the American Antiquarian Society. Catalog Record #504357," AAS, accessed July 24, 2018, http://catalog.mwa.org/vwebv/holdingsInfo?bibId=504357.

11. "General Catalog of the American Antiquarian Society. Catalog Record #505205," AAS, accessed July 24, 2018, http://catalog.mwa.org/vwebv/holdingsInfo?searchId=1657&recCount=10&recPointer=1&bibId=505205.

12. "Ambrotypes Collection Inventory," AAS, accessed July 24, 2018, http://www.americanantiquarian.org/content/ambrotypes-inventory.

13. "Daguerreotype Collection Inventory," AAS, accessed July 24, 2018, http://www.americanantiquarian.org/content/daguerreotype-inventory.

14. "The European Political Print Collection, Illustrated Box List. Box 1 Folder 1," AAS, accessed July 24, 2018, http://www.americanantiquarian.org/Inventories/Europeanprints/b1f1.htm.

15. Molly O'Hagan Hardy, "Isaiah Thomas's Broadside Ballads: Verses in Vogue with the Vulgar," *Past Is Present* (blog), January 27, 2015, accessed July 24, 2018, http://pastispresent.org/2015/digital-humanities-2/isaiah-thomass-broadside-ballads-verses-in-vogue-with-the-vulgar.

16. "From English to Algonquian: Early New England Translations," AAS, accessed July 24, 2018, http://www.americanantiquarian.org/EnglishtoAlgonquian.

17. "Mill Girls in Nineteenth-Century Print," AAS, accessed July 24, 2018, http://www.americanantiquarian.org/millgirls.

18. "The Printers' File at AAS," AAS, accessed July 24, 2018, http://www.americanantiquarian.org/printers-file.

Chapter Two

The History Project

Increasing Access to LGBT History in Boston

Samantha Strain and Peter Botticelli

The History Project (THP) offers an interesting case of a relatively small, community-based, all-volunteer archival repository that has been collecting materials actively for decades in Boston, with a mission "to document and preserve the history of Boston's LGBT community, and to share that information with the public."[1] THP emphasizes that its work aims to make visible often excluded or obscured narratives, to preserve LGBT individuals' social and historical contributions, and to increase access to the inaccessible, fragmented, and scattered history of the LGBT community. A major goal is also to provide a forum for educating the general public, so while THP is very clearly a community-centered "safe" space for LGBT individuals, it also aims to reach a more general or mainstream audience, serving an activist role in increasing the visibility of LGBT contributions through public history and storytelling based on its collections. Lately, THP has been committed to digital projects and online access to support its mission of outreach, education, and general contributions to community identity and memory building. THP recently established a digital repository featuring selected materials, and the organization is actively thinking about future directions for digital asset management.

INTERVIEWS

We gathered data on THP's history and current plans through three interviews with key volunteers, which together provided us with a wide perspective on THP's past development and future plans, including an in-depth look at digital initiatives. Andrew Elder, archivist at the University of Massachusetts, Boston, has been involved with THP since 2006; he has served on the board of trustees since 2013 and as cochair since 2016. Libby Bouvier, head of archives at the Massachusetts Supreme Judicial Court and a cofounder of THP, now serves on the board as treasurer and also sits on a subcommittee for archives and research. Finally, William Holden is a historian and writer who has worked with THP for three years, starting as a volunteer and now serving as a board member, volunteer coordinator, and chair of the subcommittee for archives and research.

HISTORY OF THP

The History Project began in 1980 as the Boston Area Lesbian and Gay History Project, organized by a group of local historians, archivists, and activists. After working to generate interest through flyers and an advertisement in the *Gay Community News* (*GCN*), a widely circulated lesbian and gay community newspaper at the time, the group began meeting at Bromfield Street Education Center, where *GCN* was headquartered. The impetus for the project was anticipation of the 350th anniversary of the founding of Boston and a desire to highlight lesbian and gay history in Massachusetts as well as the contributions of gay and lesbian individuals throughout the city's history. With the help of Harvard students and faculty, the THP founding group created a slideshow as an educational tool to help reclaim Boston's lesbian and gay history from what was largely a void in the mainstream historical record. Once finished, the slideshow was shown at gay or gay-friendly bars, as well as at local universities and colleges. Libby Bouvier recounts that many individuals whom they approached "thought there was no such thing as lesbian and gay history" and that "not every place wanted [the slideshow] or thought [it] appropriate," especially for students—resistance that underscores the lack of acceptance, understanding, and validation that THP has sought to correct.

The nascent History Project group marched in the Boston Pride Parade in June 1980 and by 1981 had officially incorporated as a 501(c)(3) nonprofit. After the 1982 arson of the Bromfield Street Education Center, the group shifted its meetings to the South End, finding space in community centers and in community members' houses. They eventually found dedicated space in the top floor of a house in Boston's Back Bay neighborhood, where the organization remains today. Beyond continued revisions and showings of its educational slideshow, the group gradually expanded its activities to include the recording of oral histories, authoring a book on LGBT individuals in Boston history, and collecting materials relating to LGBT history from community donors. In 1994, the New York Public Library (NYPL) put on a large

LGBT history exhibition to commemorate the Stonewall riots,[2] and the Boston mayor's office wanted to plan a local exhibition to complement the NYPL exhibition. The New York exhibition led to a collaboration involving THP and the Boston Public Library (BPL), which culminated in an exhibition called "Public Faces / Private Lives." A sizable increase in donations and volunteers for THP resulted. "We were always pretty much a collective," Bouvier noted, "in the sense that people really needed to work together." This sentiment holds true for the organization's current activities, which are led by a nine-member volunteer board cochaired by Andrew Elder and Joan Ilacqua, a project archivist for the Archives for Women in Medicine at the Center for the History of Medicine at Harvard Medical School. The board is a "working board," a concept articulated by multiple members as meaning that all board members do varied levels of work at THP, from high-level institutional planning and administration to hands-on processing of collections. Beyond the core group of board members, THP has between twelve and eighteen regular volunteers, a number that has quadrupled in recent years.

The History Project's collections consist largely of personal and organizational records, publications, and ephemeral materials relating to the activities of members of Boston's LGBT communities. THP also has extensive photograph collections, as well as a large collection of audiovisual materials, including the output of an oral history program. Officially, THP has a collecting policy that spans from "the Colonial period to present," although the bulk of the records date from the 1960s to the present. THP is still actively collecting materials, with new collections arriving regularly from community donors.

Beyond its core mission of collecting and making archives accessible for research, THP's mission also includes hosting public events at a growing rate of eight to twelve per year. These include THP's ongoing "Out of the Archives" lecture series, as well as events held jointly with other local nonprofits, such as the Lyric Stage Company of Boston and Historic New England. THP has also sponsored traveling and in-house exhibitions, film screenings, and a variety of publications, including a map describing historical routes of the annual Boston Pride Parade and the 1998 book titled *Improper Bostonians: Lesbian and Gay History from the Puritans to Playland*, published by Beacon Press.

DIGITAL PROJECTS

When asked how they perceived digital projects as supporting THP's mission, all interviewees identified a similar commitment to increasing access to collections online, particularly with the aim of reaching beyond the local community. William Holden cited an example of reference emails from patrons outside Boston who had discovered THP collections online. Digital access is also viewed as an important means to raise Boston's visibility in LGBT history in general. Andrew Elder explained that since "Boston is a hub for LGBT activism historically," THP's digital work can and should "expand that role's reach" beyond the city. All three interviewees, and Elder in particular, took the view that THP should not digitize its collections "for the sake of digitizing," as prior attempts at digitization had resulted in a hard drive of nested folders that were not adequately described or documented. With this lesson, THP's leadership aims to ensure that digital projects are adequately planned in advance and the resulting assets are managed more systematically, such that digitized collections will contain adequate contextual information to support access and use.

For ongoing and future digitization projects, THP plans to continue using Omeka as its primary access system. THP identifies a lack of technology infrastructure to support its own platform, though Elder indicated that as the project's digital work expands and evolves, this might change. For now, the institution sees Omeka as a good fit, as it is cost-effective and easy to learn and use; it also provides a flexible way to display objects and has the basic structure of Dublin Core to support discovery. Teachability is especially important to The History Project, as its work is completed largely by volunteers, many of whom are not archivists by training and arrive with no prior skills or experience with digitization or with metadata. Elder expressed a sense of both frustration and acceptance regarding what he sees as the need to "give up a little bit of control" in the process of digitization. Because many volunteers currently work on digital projects, THP has set minimal requirements for the metadata records contained in Omeka. These include top-level Dublin Core fields: title, unique identifier, format, file type, and rights are the only fields specifically required, while dates and personal names are added when they are known. The repository does not provide robust subject terms, a reflection of the organization's limited resources. THP clearly does not want to overburden its volunteers with complicated workflows that may act as barriers to those without archives or library science backgrounds, although THP would clearly like to operate at a higher level in supporting discovery. As collections are processed, THP does make its collection finding aids available as PDF documents in Omeka.

Currently, THP's Omeka repository includes twelve collections, the most extensive of which are the Charles Shively Collection, which was digitized through grant funding, and the Boston's Other Voice Radio Program Collection, which makes available hours of audio recordings of an LGBT radio program that ran from 1981 to 1989. Beyond Omeka, THP has worked to expand its online presence by embracing social media and its potential to provide new ways of "doing history," including the use of Facebook and

Twitter to provide information about THP events. Libby Bouvier sees the project's online presence as having grown more robust yearly. THP is also actively working to upgrade its institutional website (https://www.historyproject.org) to provide a more effective gateway for its collections. THP views the website redesign as a major opportunity to transform how it communicates with users, but like everything else at The History Project, the website is being developed as a volunteer effort by an advisory committee member with a background in web development.

CHALLENGES

When asked what factors limited THP's ability to expand its online presence, all three interviewees pointed immediately to financial constraints, as nearly 80 percent of the organization's annual budget goes to renting space in the Back Bay. No board members, cochairs, committee organizers, or volunteers are paid, except in instances where grants have funded internship positions. Closely tied to a scarcity of funds is THP's self-identified lack of people power. While the organization has dedicated volunteers who provide genuine value, their hours are often irregular, and much effort is needed to match volunteers' specific skill sets to the demands of specific projects, including digitization. A major infrastructural barrier is also the lack of technology resources, as THP owns just a few computers, most of which are used for writing finding aids and for communicating with researchers, and storage only exists in the form of external hard drives that are backed up periodically and supplemented with the use of Dropbox. THP is currently seeking to upgrade its storage and preservation methods, ideally with an in-house digital asset management system.

Another challenge for THP's digital asset management and digital initiatives is a lack of institutional documentation. Elder stated that to date THP has produced only "a couple of digital collections that were really specifically and strategically dealt with," with the result that THP owns a hard drive that contains a "terabyte of files going back to the early 2000s," representing archival materials that were scanned with the intention of providing digital access; however, they lacked consistent metadata aside from file names and the titles of the nested folders in which they resided, as well as documentation on how the records were digitized. Elder is working to sort through these materials, but he estimates that the best option will likely be to have them rescanned as part of THP's ongoing digitization activities. Elder's experience with undocumented digital assets underscores his and the other board members' commitment to intentional planning as part of THP's digital strategy.

In pursuing digital projects, THP has received a number of grants, including funding through the Massachusetts Foundation for the Humanities, which supported the processing and digitization of the Charles Shively Collection. Through its experience with small digitization grants for specific collections, THP aims to apply for more, perhaps larger, grants in the future. Another Massachusetts Foundation for the Humanities grant has provided funding to digitize sixteen albums containing obituaries of HIV/AIDS victims. Created by a community member and donated to The History Project in the 1990s, this collection of newspaper clippings memorializing victims of the AIDS crisis was chosen for the grant due to the immediate preservation concerns around print newspapers. By digitizing these objects, THP aims to capture the layout of the pages (on which clippings are organized alphabetically), as well as to digitize each item individually. This project has inherent privacy concerns, as the albums were created by a community member and the individuals represented therein may not have known they were included and could not have anticipated the clippings' being made accessible to a wider audience online. In order to respect the privacy of all individuals represented, THP has decided to proceed with the digitization of all the obituaries, but in the case of those that do not specifically identify an individual as having died of HIV/AIDS, THP will make a redacted version publicly accessible.

COLLABORATIONS

Given the scope of its ambitions and also its limited resources, THP has actively sought to collaborate with larger organizations, including Northeastern University Libraries' Archives and Special Collections. At one time, THP had considered a formal affiliation with Northeastern, which has had a focus on documenting underrepresented groups in Boston, including LGBT communities. But wary of being subsumed by a larger institution, THP opted to keep its independence and instead to collaborate on specific projects. Bouvier, for one, worried that THP's mission might be subject to university administrations' changing desires and that Northeastern could put up undue barriers to access and the free use of THP's collections. Still, both Bouvier and Elder indicated that THP and Northeastern University Libraries have been able to collaborate in mutually beneficial ways in recent years. Northeastern has encouraged donors to consider THP in cases where the library has encountered materials it felt belonged in the more community-oriented space of THP, and The History Project has likewise pointed donors to Northeastern for materials that it may be better equipped to handle, including records with sensitive personal information (e.g., medical patient records) that call for stringent access restrictions.

In seeking to move beyond short-term, project-based collaborations, THP recently began to investigate the possibility of a longer-term partnership with the Digital Commonwealth, a consortium of library, archives, and museum institutions in Massachusetts that has received state funding to digitize cultural heritage materials and to make them accessible online through its own portal and through the Digital Public Library of America. THP sees the Digital Commonwealth as a potential opportunity to greatly increase access to its collections, going well beyond the limited capabilities of its Omeka site. As an example, THP is exploring the possibility of making the *Gay Community News* collection available through the Digital Commonwealth. *GCN* was a community newspaper published weekly from 1973 to 1992 and then on a quarterly basis until 1999. Previously, THP has worked with the Northeastern University Libraries to make *GCN* available digitally. THP helped Northeastern acquire a nearly complete run of *GCN*, and later Northeastern made the full text of the digitized publication available through ProQuest. However, THP would like to provide a higher level of access than was possible with Northeastern's digitization of *GCN*, which captured a text-only version of the publication, and the resource was made accessible only to registered users of Northeastern University Libraries. By working with the Digital Commonwealth, Bouvier is hopeful that THP could make page images of the newspaper available to the public, including such items as personal ads and letters to the editor that were excluded by Northeastern in its original digitization effort. THP's collection includes microfilm copies of the publication from 1973 to 1988, while the Boston Public Library—a Digital Commonwealth member and the site of its digitization lab—has a complete run from 1973 to 1999. In addition to the newspaper itself, THP is interested in making available its collection of *GCN* staff photographs, and discussions with the Digital Commonwealth have indicated that if THP were to provide basic metadata and copyright information for these images, they could be digitized and made accessible through the Digital Commonwealth portal. In general, THP recognizes the inevitable "growing pains" as it expands its digital collections and works to gain better control over its digital assets. The organization sees this as a priority to further develop its collection documentation and to set formal digitization policies and clear workflows in order to simplify training for volunteers while at the same time ensuring consistency in the output of digital projects.

CONCLUSION

Bouvier and Elder both expressed a desire for THP to provide a wider and more comprehensive view of the LGBT community than before, as in the past the organization has tended to focus on documenting the experiences of gay white males. Elder commented, "I don't think about amount. I don't care about how many things we digitize. I care about digitizing things that are useful for researchers" and "doing work that is meaningful" and "representative of our community." In working to "digitize collections that represent different communities within our already underrepresented community," Elder hopes to draw attention to "who is missing" from collections and to make "really smart decisions" in digital curation selection that "our community can be proud of."

NOTES

1. The History Project, accessed August 8, 2018, https://www.historyproject.org.
2. The Stonewall riots were confrontations between police and members of the gay community in Greenwich Village in 1969; they are now regarded as a milestone in the gay rights movement.

Chapter Three

Historic New England

Building a Complex Infrastructure

Peter Botticelli, Martha R. Mahard,
Michèle V. Cloonan, and Brett Freiburger

Historic New England (HNE) describes itself as "the oldest and largest regional heritage organization in the nation." It was founded in 1910 as the Society for the Preservation of New England Antiquities by William Sumner Appleton, a pioneering historic preservationist who clearly understood the value of documentation in preserving historic buildings and landscapes. He was a determined collector with eclectic tastes and a passion for objects reflecting daily life in New England, with the result that by the 1940s, the society had accumulated roughly fifty historic properties, along with museum and library collections consisting of over half a million total objects. Today, HNE's collections include 37 sites and 160 buildings scattered across the region, plus 120,000 museum objects and 1.5 million archival records. Photographs are the single most common object type, with nearly half a million images, but the collections include such varied objects as wallpaper, jewelry, musical instruments, account books, architectural drawings, farm implements, manuscripts, and personal papers. According to Senior Curator of Libraries and Archives Lorna Condon, one of our interviewees, "The ideal property comes to HNE intact," with the decorative arts, furniture, personal papers, and so forth, that make a house and its contents an authentic representation of the people who lived there. Once HNE acquires a property, highly valuable objects may be removed and kept in the society's main storage facility; yet many original objects are kept in their original setting. Archival materials are generally removed to facilitate processing and use by researchers, but even so, as a library, archives, and museum (LAM) institution, HNE maintains a strong connection to the built environment as an essential part of New England's social history.

INTERVIEWS

Given our particular focus on the role of library and archival collections within HNE, we interviewed both Lorna Condon (as noted above) and David Dwiggins, who currently serves as HNE's information technology officer. HNE was one of the partner institutions with whom we collaborated on the 2009–2012 Institute of Museum and Library Services grant project.[1] During the project we focused on work at the Gropius House in Lincoln, Massachusetts, and gained insights into the complications involved in bringing a historic house into the institutional network, at the same time describing objects and the book collection in the house library.

BACKGROUND

As LAM educators, we have long been intrigued by the complex, highly eclectic nature of HNE's collections, which present distinct challenges as well as opportunities for curating this unique and valuable slice of material culture. As an organization, HNE offers a useful case example of a collecting institution that has long functioned as a well-integrated hybrid, successfully combining the elements of a museum, a library and archives, and a historical society with a focus on preservation. Appleton himself made a point of establishing the library and archives as a core part of the society's mission. This history has made HNE a particularly valuable site for internships.

DIGITAL INITIATIVES

With the range and depth of its collections, HNE clearly has great potential to expand the scope of its audience engagement activities by digitizing collection materials, building upon HNE's well-established public identity as a destination for historic sites. In recent years, HNE has taken important steps toward building its digital capacity, both for creating digital surrogates and for providing online access to the collections. At the same time, HNE has worked to address the urgent need to use technology to better manage the large volume of paper and born-digital records that are used to document the society's extensive preservation activities. In this context, we view HNE as a case example of a LAM that has been successful in leveraging available (limited, that is) resources to make real inroads in managing its growing volume of digital assets of all types.

A turning point for HNE's digital initiatives occurred in 2008, when Condon successfully argued for the hiring of a systems librarian/archivist within the Collection Services unit; David Dwiggins was the person brought on to fill this role. For Dwiggins, the job began as a challenge, particularly as HNE's sprawling mission and resource constraints made information technology a "relatively low priority on the institutional totem pole," in his words. Nevertheless, Dwiggins found that by working on the organization's periphery, his technology-focused role afforded a genuine opportunity to be innovative in building HNE's digital infrastructure. In fact, Dwiggins's arrival at HNE coincided with the grant-funded Collections Access Project (CAP), a multiyear effort to scale up HNE's digitization and metadata creation activities, as well as the aim of implementing a new collections management system (CMS) along with a revamped public website. Previously, the library and archives had relied on text-based finding aids for discovery—a less than optimal solution for web-based discovery. In choosing a CMS, Condon noted that largely due to limited funds, HNE wanted a single system with all the capabilities needed to manage LAM collections. This led HNE to choose a proprietary system that included a library and archives module along with the functionality needed for museum collections. As became clear later on, the choice of CMS involved a number of trade-offs. For one, the new CMS proved to be not nearly as "out of the box" as hoped at the outset—over time much customization was required to make the system function properly. In working with the CMS, Dwiggins also encountered roadblocks in the varied nature of the digital assets being managed; for instance, the previous adoption of different numbering systems and varying descriptive standards for the different collection types led to inefficiencies in managing HNE's growing volume of digital assets.

RESOURCESPACE REPOSITORY

Ultimately Dwiggins saw the need for a digital asset management (DAM) system, in addition to the CMS, to enable HNE to properly store and manage the complete range of digital assets that were being created using HNE's newly enhanced on-site digitization capabilities. From a LAM perspective, it is significant that Dwiggins, acting as part of a relatively small team, was given substantial latitude in evaluating and selecting a DAM technology that would eventually be used across the whole organization. Given his background in working with information technology, Dwiggins was drawn to ResourceSpace as an open source application that would allow "under-the-hood" adjustments as needed and be compatible with other open source "helper" applications that could be used to perform such functions as creating thumbnail images, adding geolocation tags, and exporting database reports.

Still, as Dwiggins is quick to point out, open source software is "free like puppies," meaning that while it is free to install, system maintenance and upgrades entail substantial costs over time. In effect, by choosing an open source application to work alongside HNE's proprietary CMS, Dwiggins was able to experiment with a DAM technology without the organization having to commit substantial resources from the outset.

Dwiggins had the ResourceSpace repository running by mid-2009 with a limited number of registered users—Dwiggins himself along with a few selected members of HNE's Collection Services and Property Care teams. Dwiggins's strategy was to avoid forcing the use of ResourceSpace and instead to encourage different units at HNE to adopt it organically, as they came to see how it might complement or enhance their existing workflows. This soft approach to the rollout of ResourceSpace proved successful, leading to a slow but steady increase in use by staff and in the number of digital resources in the system. By the end of 2010, HNE had gone from a few dozen new resources added per month, on average, to a few hundred. To date, the Property Care and Collection Services teams have each added over one hundred thousand individual resources, which generally include one or more master images showing different views of the subject, plus derivatives used for access purposes. Within a few years, HNE had a few terabytes of data in ResourceSpace, out of the estimated twenty to thirty terabytes stored on various devices (e.g., servers, DVDs) at HNE.

By 2013, Dwiggins had taken on an expanded role as HNE's information technology officer, with responsibility for overseeing the management of digital assets and systems across the institution. In this role, Dwiggins had to ensure that the technology in use matched the varied workflows across HNE. Part of the success of ResourceSpace was due to its interoperability with the existing CMS, enabling users to navigate easily between metadata records in the CMS and digital surrogates stored in the ResourceSpace repository. For instance, the Property Care team focused on resources for internal use in maintaining the sites, while the Collection Services unit directly concerned itself with public access to digitized material from the library, archives, and museum collections, for which descriptive metadata and search features need to be tailored for external users. As these units were the earliest adopters of ResourceSpace at HNE, Dwiggins found himself in a good position to observe how the repository might be optimized for HNE's internal workflows as well as to support public access.

NEW PROJECTS

In general, HNE has been moving toward a more centralized model for managing digital assets, with the aim of facilitating access to and new uses of assets across different units. For example, HNE has recently been carrying out a major project involving the Eustis House in Milton, Massachusetts. This site represents a new chapter in digitization for HNE because the project involves high-resolution 3-D imaging of the house exterior and interior and the gardens. The Property Care team originated the 3-D imaging project as part of its preservation work; yet the large volume of visual data has many potential uses, including the development of a virtual tour. Also, as this is a recently acquired HNE property, the development, marketing, and publications departments are interested in using images of the estate. Lorna Condon describes public access to collections as revolutionary for HNE, as the ability to search across museum, library, and archives collections through a single system has changed user expectations and, by extension, the public perception of HNE as an institution.

CONCLUSION

Over the past decade, digital initiatives have succeeded in building up HNE's technology infrastructure, laying the groundwork for additional collaboration between disciplines. The success of the underlying infrastructure can be seen in the sophisticated, user-friendly collection searching available on its website, making HNE's rich and varied collections accessible to a global audience.

NOTE

1. IMLS Grant, Laura Bush 21st Century Librarian Program, RE-05-09-0082-09, "Curriculum, Cooperation, Convergence, Capacity: 4Cs for the Development of Cultural Heritage Institutions: Libraries, Museums, and Archives in the Twenty-First Century," 2009–2012, accessed August 11, 2018, https://www.imls.gov/grants/awarded/re-05-09-0082-09.

Chapter Four

The Maine Memory Network

A Statewide Collaboration

Peter Botticelli and Emeline Dehn-Reynolds

The Maine Historical Society (MHS), located in Portland, Maine, was founded in 1822. It is the third-oldest historical society in the United States, with about twenty-five hundred members. Currently employing thirty-five full- and part-time staff members, it consists of four parts: the Wordsworth-Longfellow House, the Maine Historical Society Museum and Store, the Brown Research Library, and the web-based Maine Memory Network (MMN). The organization has published the peer-reviewed journal *Maine History* since 1961 and continues to add to its collection of over sixty published monographs. For this case study we were interested in the development of a complex statewide collaborative online resource.

INTERVIEWS

With data provided by MHS, we were able to examine how MMN has developed over time, including its funding, personnel, and technology infrastructure. Two of the MHS staff members are primarily dedicated to MMN. Kathy Amoroso, MHS director of digital engagement, began in 2001 as outreach coordinator and is now the senior staff member responsible for MMN. Her duties include working with image donors, curating the images and metadata that appear online, staff and volunteer supervision, IT troubleshooting, and communications with MMN partners. Tilly Laskey serves as MHS outreach coordinator and creates online exhibits for MMN as well as physical exhibits displayed in the MHS library. She also recruits and helps train new contributors to MMN. The staff of MHS's Brown Research Library provide some additional support, including scanning and metadata creation for items originating in the MHS collections. MHS also employs a web developer as an independent hourly contractor. This individual has worked with MMN for several years and has been largely responsible for building the architecture, aesthetics, and functionality of the MMN sites. The web developer works closely with Kathy Amoroso to ensure that MMN's coding and functionality are stable, scalable, and current.

HISTORY OF MMN

The Maine Memory Network was established in 1999 in response to the Maine Legislature's Maine Communities in the New Century Program, which aimed to better preserve and improve public access to local and statewide historical resources. Seed funding from the New Century Program allowed for the creation of the Maine Network Partners, a coalition of seven organizations: Folger Library at the University of Maine at Orono, the Northeast Historical Film Preservation Commission, the Maine Humanities Council, the Maine State Library, the Maine State Museum, the Osher Map Library (University of Southern Maine at Portland), and the Maine Historical Society in Portland. After a prototype was developed, MMN went live in September 2001 with material from the MHS and several other institutions, making MMN one of the first statewide publicly accessible digital archives in the United States. MMN's stated mission is to partner with all of Maine's cultural institutions to document the state's heritage. MMN has since grown to include over forty-five thousand images, and the site averages about twenty-five thousand visitors per month. MMN includes online exhibits such as "400 Years of New Mainers" and Maine History Online, an interactive history of Maine from 1500 to the present, grouped by theme and period. An innovative aspect of MMN consists of the "Mystery Corner," whereby certain images that are missing contextual information can be tagged for review by the general public. This strategy has proven very successful for some images. "My Maine Stories" is the newest branch of the MMN; it features an interactive service whereby users can submit their own "Maine stories." Suggested subject areas include "Millworkers," "GLBTQ Mainers," and "Wabanaki People" stories.

In its early years, MMN had roughly one hundred contributors from across the state. Two decades later, that number had more than tripled, and MMN itself had grown to include four separate websites: the Maine Memory Network, Vintage Maine Images (VMI), the Longfellow Poem Database, and the Maine Historical Society site. For these online resources, MMN acts as a digital asset management system as well as an online portal to an open and searchable database of digitized images that originate with the MHS collections, other partner institutions in the state, and, more recently, individuals with a connection to Maine's history and culture. The Maine Historical Society website was established in 2000 as the front page for the historical society, including information on events, news, podcasts, and catalogs of the Brown Research Library and MHS museum holdings. MHS members are given full-text access to the journal *Maine History*, among other library resources. The VMI database, also established in 2000, offers eleven thousand images and metadata drawn from the same database as the Maine Memory Network. VMI receives approximately six thousand visitors per month. For prices ranging from $15 to $275, individuals and nonprofit/for-profit groups can order high-quality reproductions and license digital or paper photo reproductions. The Longfellow Poem Database, established in 2005, presents biographical material and a searchable database of every known poem by Henry Wadsworth Longfellow.

FUNDING AND IMPLEMENTATION OF THE NETWORK

From the outset, MMN has been funded primarily by grants, beginning with initial seed funding from the state legislature in 2000. The most significant contributor to date has been the Institute of Museum and Library Services, which has awarded MHS eleven grants worth over $2.5 million between 2002 and 2016, with nine grants totaling just over $2 million specifically earmarked for MMN. Other contributors to MMN have included the National Endowment for the Humanities and a number of private foundations. A small amount has come from the Maine Historical Society itself, and the Vintage Maine Images site is self-funding through user fees.

The ongoing cost of maintaining MMN's infrastructure and essential services is roughly $20,000 per year. This does not include significant onetime costs for upgrades or new functionality, including the recent addition of the "My Maine Stories" public contribution site. In the past, MMN has relied on grants to cover equipment costs, which now include monthly subscription fees for cloud-based storage. MMN's heavy reliance on grants has placed constraints on what can be done to expand the service and ensure its long-term sustainability, with the result that MHS's fund-raising staff have begun to consider other options, such as corporate sponsorship and online advertising, should grant funding become scarcer in the future.

To date, about half of the forty-five thousand total images in MMN represent MHS collections; yet these account for less than 1 percent of MHS holdings. Otherwise, nearly three hundred cultural heritage institutions have contributed some or many images to MMN. Amoroso notes that only about five institutions are active contributors at any given time. She estimates the potential number of eligible Maine cultural heritage institutions to be closer to nine hundred. The *Contributing Partners' Manual* lists "historical societies, museums, and libraries" as eligible candidates, though a range of other organizations, such as the Maine Department of Transportation, the Maine Forest Service, the City of Brewer, and Portland's Congregation Shaarey Tphiloh, have also contributed to MMN. MHS offers comprehensive guidance to contributors in selecting, digitizing, describing, and uploading materials for free access through the MMN site or for a fee through the Vintage Maine Images site. MMN uses modified Dublin Core elements for basic metadata, including title, location, dimensions, and so forth, along with MMN's own set of subject categories as well as Library of Congress subject headings. Digital surrogates and accompanying metadata are produced by partner institutions and then uploaded directly to the MMN site. Before images are made publicly accessible on MMN, MHS staff review them for quality, subject, and completeness of metadata. This "hands-on" approach means that every single publicly available image has been reviewed by MHS staff to ensure that the content meets MMN's standards for online display.

CHALLENGES OF STATEWIDE COLLABORATION

For MHS staff, working with contributors has been complicated by Maine's geography and climate as well as its history, which has produced a cultural landscape consisting of many small and widely scattered museums and historical societies that are open only during the summer and frequently run by volunteers, including many seasonal residents. At the same time, many smaller institutions lack the equipment and technical capabilities needed to contribute to MMN, and those willing and able to contribute often need training and support to meet MMN's image-quality and metadata guidelines. MHS staff have developed several solutions to these difficulties. In the spring, Amoroso calls town offices and libraries for revised contact information and to suggest funding options for purchasing equipment. As much as possible, she makes in-person visits to provide technical support, and a number of contributing institutions (e.g., South Berwick Historical Society) have worked with local schools to pair the technological expertise of the younger generation with the historical knowledge of the elder ones. Due to current grant requirements, MHS has begun to focus more on recruiting and training individual content donors ("formal individual contributors") rather than raising the number of participating institutions. Amoroso is optimistic about working more directly with individuals, although she acknowledges that problems with image-quality control, intellectual property compliance, and computer literacy may increase with the higher number of donors involved. Cindi Young-Gomes, formerly a curator at Museums of Old York (York, Maine), recalls a "learning curve" when her institution began uploading images to MMN. Between 2006 and 2013, Old York managed to upload forty-two images. Most were of larger objects, such as furniture, which required Young-Gomes to use a digital camera and available lighting, although some smaller objects could be digitized with a flatbed scanner. The digital surrogates were then loaded into the museum's PastPerfect database and assigned metadata by Young-Gomes. A student intern from Berwick Academy (South Berwick, Maine) then uploaded the images to MMN along with item-level metadata copied from PastPerfect.

Once uploaded, digital images and metadata are stored in a series of MySQL databases, with one database assigned to each of the four public websites administered by MHS (Longfellow Poem Database, Maine Historical Society, Vintage Maine Images, and Maine Memory Network), along with supporting databases used for related functions such as tracking who has access to various website functions, usage statistics, and so forth. Until 2015–2016, the MMN databases were hosted on in-house servers, which were also used to back up all MHS-created files. Contributing partner institutions maintain their own backups and websites separate from the MHS system. Recently, Amoroso and the MHS administration made the decision to outsource web hosting and some online storage to third-party vendors. This change was made at the suggestion of the MMN web developer, who was concerned about the increasing hardware age within MHS's IT infrastructure. MHS has also incorporated social media platforms such as Facebook, Twitter, and Pinterest, and MHS staff routinely use Google Analytics to track website usage trends, although Amoroso notes that content submission from both MHS and contributing partner organizations has been driven much less by usage trends than by grants, themed exhibits, and commemorative events for state institutions.

THE FUTURE

Several new features of MMN are planned. One will allow related images to appear at the bottom of an image's entry. Another tool will enable users to create their own exhibits by gathering together items from the MMN collection. There are plans to help small institutions create customized image exhibits for display to complement their physical exhibits and expand public awareness of the MMN holdings. MHS staff hope these interactive features will be useful for educators, historical societies, and the general public. As MHS plans for the future, a key technology goal is to implement a single, comprehensive digital asset management system to support all of its existing websites, while maintaining much of the current functionality in the sites, including support for existing file formats, metadata schemas, exhibit building, Americans with Disabilities Act compliance, and interactive features for patron comments and image licensing. MHS would like to continue using as many open source applications as possible, and it needs to support multiple access levels, assigning MHS administrators higher privileges than contributing partner staff in order to properly curate content and giving MHS effective control over backend functions of the system.

CONCLUSION

If its future is anything like its accomplishments so far, the Maine Memory Network will continue to serve as a vital and indispensable source for thousands of people across Maine and beyond. Since its founding in 1999, it has actively supported a wide range of digitization projects by cultural heritage institutions in the state. Despite the challenges, including technology, geography, and collaboration across institutional boundaries, MMN has flourished as a platform for presenting the history and experience of Mainers in their own words and images.

Part II

Collaboration within and across Institutions

Chapter Five

The American Archive of Public Broadcasting

Media Access and Preservation

Peter Botticelli, Bryce Roe, and Lily Troia

The Corporation for Public Broadcasting (CPB) was established in 1967 to support public media across the United States. Public radio and television stations had existed since the 1920s, but the formation of the CPB led to a proliferation of media outlets and a large increase in content documenting American society and culture. The decentralized structure of public broadcasting in the United States gave local stations effective control over production decisions and sole authority for program selection and scheduling. The result was a siloed production model lacking standardization in archival management, and with perennially limited resources, public broadcasters tended to favor production over preservation, leaving much public media content at risk.[1] To address preservation needs for public media, in 2013 CPB fostered a partnership between Boston's WGBH—one of the largest public television and radio broadcasters and content producers in the United States—and the Library of Congress (LOC). The result was the American Archive of Public Broadcasting (AAPB), a collaborative effort that aims "to preserve and make accessible significant historical content created by public media, and to coordinate a national effort to save at-risk public media before its content is lost to posterity," according to Alan Gevinson, LOC project director.

INTERVIEWS

In studying AAPB, we aimed to assess audiovisual preservation and data management methods currently used in the public media sector, to examine AAPB's digital content management systems and workflows, and to investigate the organizational dynamics and sustainability of a large-scale collaboration in the cultural heritage sector. We gathered the bulk of our data through nine interviews at WGBH and LOC with personnel responsible for information technology, systems development and analysis, metadata implementation, ingestion and quality control, stock sales and licensing, and project management. Our WGBH interviewees included Karen Cariani, project director; Casey Davis, project manager; Drew Meyers, senior developer; Chuck McCallum, developer; Kevin Carter, programmer/systems analyst; Rebecca Fraimow, archivist/National Digital Stewardship Residency coordinator; and Sadie Roosa, archivist/metadata specialist. At LOC, we interviewed Rachel Curtis, digital conversion specialist, along with Project Director Alan Gevinson.

PRESERVATION EFFORTS

AAPB has its roots in a succession of preservation efforts that began in 2004 with the Preserving Digital Public Television (PDPTV) Project, which was part of the LOC-administered National Digital Information and Infrastructure Program (NDIIP). As a collaboration between WGBH, PBS, New York University, and WNET (a large public broadcaster and content producer based in New York), PDPTV assessed the challenges of preserving born-digital media content. This effort paved the way for CPB's American Archive initiative, which began in 2007 as an outcome of PBS's conversion from analog to digital transmission. In 2009, CPB launched a pilot project in which Oregon Public Broadcasting was given funding to digitize twenty-five hundred hours of vulnerable public radio and television assets relating to civil rights activities or World War II veterans, as a venue for exploring best practices for metadata, analog-to-digital workflows, preservation, rights and permissions, and online access to digital content. CPB went on to sponsor the digitization of an additional forty thousand hours of television and radio assets from over 120 stations nationwide. Each station chose the programming to be digitized; in many cases, they selected assets considered to be at high risk, including those in legacy formats and with minimal descriptive metadata available. WGBH itself opted to digitize a large collection of quarter-inch audio that contained rare examples of early radio programs. Most stations selected local programming considered historically significant to their communities, including some material they hoped to relicense and monetize. In 2010, CPB chose WGBH to coordinate the American Archive Content Inventory Project (CIP), which funded the creation of inventory records of the holdings of 120 public media stations, which were then aggregated and managed directly by WGBH. Between 2010 and 2012, WGBH acquired 2.5 million asset-level inventory records, far exceeding the CPB's initial estimate of 100,000 records. WGBH developed a content management system for the CIP metadata, which was encoded with a modified version of the PBCore schema. This homegrown system eventually became the core digital asset management (DAM) infrastructure for AAPB.

PERMANENT ENTITY GRANT

A turning point came in 2012, when CPB lost its digital projects funding from Congress; this made the sustainability of existing digital assets a critical issue, according to Karen Cariani. With the conclusion of the American Archive project, in 2013 CPB chose WGBH and LOC as partners in the Permanent Entity Grant, which came to be known as Phase I of AAPB. In addition to being a large producer of public media content, WGBH brought its experience as the first public media station to establish a formal archives back in 1979, while LOC has long been a source of expertise in the preservation of time-based media. AAPB was established with a collaborative model of governance and a common vision, but each organization took on a distinct role, with WGBH responsible for access and LOC for long-term preservation. While the teams manage their responsibilities independently, Cariani and Gevinson describe a cooperative approach to long-term strategic planning, including the development of policies and procedures, fund-raising, sustainability, collection development, and outreach initiatives. They envision the AAPB as a centralized, access-focused, user-friendly web portal for public broadcasting materials.

In 2015, Phase I of AAPB was completed, with WGBH overseeing the launch of an online reading room featuring streaming content available for on- or off-site viewing, depending on the access rights of each asset. Initially it provided access to the 2.5 million inventory records created during the CIP and highlighted selected content provided by public media outlets. Since 2015, over twelve thousand assets have been made accessible for public streaming in the Online Reading Room, and scholars and AAPB staff have curated a number of audio and video collections on topics of historical significance. WGBH's web developers, Chuck McCallum and Drew Meyers, drew upon their experiences working on WGBH's own access portal, OpenVault, and their involvement in Project Hydra, which is responsible for an open source content management system. To date, roughly 20 percent of the

AAPB's total collection has been made available online, with more content being added regularly.

Rights clearance has required obtaining permissions from originating stations and rights holders, identifying public domain materials, and exercising U.S. copyright law exceptions, including fair use, the library/archive exceptions, and existing provisions unique to public television and to LOC. AAPB assigns one of three basic web access levels. The first encompasses public domain materials and materials for which the AAPB has obtained full access permission. The second includes materials the legal team has deemed shareable for educational and scholarly purposes; these materials can be streamed on-site at WGBH and at LOC, a determination made after a careful risk assessment. The third level covers assets under review or those restricted from public access. Importantly, contributing stations are asked to license digital files to AAPB, with the option to use a creative commons license, but they are not required to sign over the copyright to the digital files they contribute.

WORKING WITH AFFILIATES

WGBH actively manages relationships with the over one hundred CPB-affiliated public media outlets, representing most U.S. states, which have contributed material to AAPB. This includes coordinating workflows whereby content is acquired from a number of digitization vendors employed by local outlets. From WGBH's perspective, the need to familiarize numerous vendors with AAPB has contributed to the project's long-term sustainability. For Casey Davis, "It is a good thing to work with multiple vendors so we can become flexible and have our workflows understood by a variety of organizations. Hopefully we will continue to grow our collections in the future, and we will have worked with different vendors over that time." Communicating with the large and varied number of AAPB participants has allowed WGBH to build valued relationships with stakeholders and to better understand the public broadcasting community's digital preservation practices and concerns. With this knowledge, WGBH hopes to streamline acquisition processes over time and eventually to allow stations to submit data to AAPB's homegrown Archival Management System. This system grew out of an open-source system that was originally built to manage inventory records for the CIP project and was later customized with web-based tools for uploading assets as they are digitized, while also delivering streaming proxy files, as noted by Kevin Carter.

PBCORE

AAPB uses PBCore (Public Broadcasting Metadata Dictionary) to support faceted browsing, searching, and discovery. The public broadcasting community originally developed PBCore in 2001 as an XML schema for public broadcasters to use in managing audiovisual assets with descriptive as well as technical metadata, which enables the exchange of data between media collections, systems, and organizations. Since then, PBCore has been widely adopted by archives with media collections, but, as Rebecca Fraimow notes, it has not yet been embraced by public media stations in large numbers. The CIP project initially had to focus on normalizing the often scant metadata submitted by stations, including formatting dates and titles as well as formatting the existing data in CSV before it could be mapped to PBCore. The next step for AAPB was to catalog the forty thousand hours' worth of content as it was digitized. In 2015, Sadie Roosa began by setting PBCore cataloging guidelines, including required and recommended elements and attributes, with controlled vocabularies reflecting the types of content likely to be included in the AAPB collection. Roosa then worked with library and information science student interns to catalog the digitized content. Due to the size and scope of the collection, the team focused on performing minimal viable cataloging (MVC) of all content, which includes asset type, title, short description, genre, asset date, creators, contributors, and a rights statement if known. Over the past two years, thirteen interns have cataloged approximately two thousand items from the collection. Following MVC's fifteen-minute-per-record guidelines, Roosa expects it to take six years to catalog the entire collection at this level and many more years to complete full records. AAPB aims to increase usage of the PBCore metadata standard through outreach to contributing stations and independent production teams and by contributing to plans for controlled vocabularies, RDF workflows, and development of tools to automatically generate PBCore records.

THE ONLINE READING ROOM

At the time it was launched, the AAPB Online Reading Room included three multimedia exhibits with rights clearances allowing for off-site streaming: "Documenting and Celebrating Public Broadcasting Station Histories," "Voices from the Southern Civil Rights Movement," and "Climate Change Conversations: Causes, Impacts, Solutions." The exhibits are organized by topic and given a narrative structure, and they are searchable within the AAPB interface, enabling them to act as starting points for deeper discovery within the repository. They feature historically significant content unearthed by interns and staff in the course of cataloging and providing access to the collection, and AAPB plans to add more exhibits with newly acquired content and with timely subject matter. Recently, for example, the AAPB launched a fourth exhibit, titled "Voices of Democracy: Public Media and Presidential Elections," which coincided with an extensive donation of New Hampshire Public Radio recordings during the 2016 general election primaries.

MANAGING ANALOG AND DIGITAL FORMATS

Over the years, public media outlets have used a wide range of analog formats; many have become obsolete before the industry has been able to migrate content to new media, according to Davis and Fraimow. Audiovisual materials are volatile by nature, with intricate file structures that often include multiple channels of audio and video, along with technical metadata such as timecodes, time-based metadata like subtitles, and descriptive metadata as well. Digital time-based media assets pose additional preservation challenges, including a lack of metadata, technology obsolescence events, and the need for item-level quality control.

Near the end of Phase I, WGBH tasked Rebecca Fraimow (then a National Digital Stewardship Resident) with facilitating the re-ingesting of digital content as part of a migration to a new DAM system. As this process took place, Fraimow notes, WGBH discovered that files were failing at an 80 percent rate, with visible errors appearing in some and others entirely unreadable. Fraimow acknowledges the trial-and-error aspect of audiovisual digital preservation as a new field in which archivists often have to invent their own solutions. Prior to joining WGBH, Fraimow was a transfer manager working on digitization, reformatting, and digital file management for the Dance Heritage Coalition, with previous experience in the development and use of open source tools for audiovisual digital preservation.

To successfully migrate the files, the WGBH team first needed to develop a process to retrieve them and to fill in gaps in the existing technical metadata, which in the past had been kept separately from the files themselves. For instance, many files lacked checksums or other file fixity information. To solve the problem, Fraimow and Carter combined a number of open source microservices, including scripts, that enabled them to identify duplicate assets, to pull available technical metadata into a PBCore-compliant XML file, and to match files with checksums using automated workflows. Fraimow describes the inherent modularity of software microservices as ideal for supporting the iterative nature of digital preservation workflows by isolating individual tasks into distinct applications that can be adjusted or upgraded without overhauling the whole system. As Fraimow explains it, "We discovered problems as we went along" in re-ingesting the files. "My process was evolving as I went, so not everything looked the same from beginning to end."

THE FUTURE

Going forward, AAPB hopes to include local production teams more directly in the preservation process. Given the rate at which daily radio and news programming is producing digital content, collaboration will be required to support the level of automation that is needed for AAPB to ingest digital assets. Fraimow emphasizes that AAPB's digital preservation workflows will always "be a living document," as preservation needs and AAPB itself continue to evolve. As a collaborative effort involving hundreds of organizations, AAPB has made outreach to stakeholders a central focus of its strategy for building the archive. Most importantly, throughout Phase I, the WGBH and LOC teams were in regular email and phone communication, with monthly virtual meetings scheduled to ensure project participants maintained awareness despite the geographical distance. While the LOC's preservation focus and WGBH's attention to access might seem divergent, or even to reflect potentially opposing needs, AAPB has managed to strike a balance between preservation and access. "We really do complement each other," says Cariani. "I'm pushing him [Gevinson] in this direction and he's pushing me in that direction—and it works!"

The AAPB leaders all express a clear need for digital preservation standards to be implemented by independent media stations and producers. As Gevinson notes, LOC has well-developed preservation plans that include keeping abreast of the latest developments and recommendations in digital preservation and reassessing preservation workflows and infrastructure as technology changes. For example, LOC has established BagIt specifications for the submission of preservation metadata directly from digitization vendors into LOC's MAVIS database, from which metadata is shared with AAPB's AMS database, as Rachel Curtis explains.

Since the conclusion of Phase I in 2015, WGBH has continued to focus on increasing access to digitized content through the AAPB Online Reading Room, while LOC has maintained its responsibility for long-term preservation. Currently, all new acquisitions must be born-digital, previously digitized by the contributing station, or digitized through grants, including a recent CLIR grant through which WGBH and WETA (based in Washington, DC) will digitize over three decades of *PBS NewsHour* broadcasts, with the content to be added to AAPB. According to Gevinson, "We want the AAPB to be a centralized web portal . . . able to direct researchers and the general public to materials," even as some public media outlets may opt to provide access through their own web portals. In some cases, AAPB may be given access copies and metadata or just metadata records with links out to content streamed from the outlet's own website. This strategy has been successful, with AAPB adding tens of thousands of hours' worth of content in recent years. Nonetheless, AAPB still has much room for growth, having identified "more than three million public broadcasting assets nationwide," according to Davis. To expand the repository further, AAPB is targeting particular collections to fill gaps in AAPB's holdings, which currently include recorded sound materials from twenty-six states and moving image materials from thirty-eight. Besides filling gaps in geography, AAPB plans to assess current holdings in an effort to identify major historical events or issues that may now be underrepresented, as well as to increase coverage of children's programming and materials produced by minority groups. Also, Cariani is interested in acquiring more content from independent producers and organizations that may be temporarily providing homes for archival audiovisual materials.

In the future, Cariani would like to see broad uses of AAPB content in education, particularly in K–12 classrooms: "I think many people learn from seeing and hearing. It is very tactile, very responsive, and it is something you can relate to." To make better use of AAPB's assets, plans are underway to develop and launch additional thematic exhibits, recognizing the potential of AAPB to reach new audiences online. Cariani notes that developing exhibits also allows AAPB to streamline the rights-clearance process by seeking permission for assets that fit particular themes, as opposed to seeking permission to digitize random buckets of assets. Gevinson emphasizes that funding organizations are more likely to support digitization projects that can provide access to the widest possible audience, making it important to target assets for which AAPB can gain access permission.

In addition to expanding the repository and widening access, Cariani and Gevinson are working to move beyond AAPB's initial reliance on short-term, project-based grant funding and ultimately to make it a sustainable entity independent of WGBH and LOC. With foundation support, they hope to build a consortium to support a five- to ten-year capacity-building effort, during which time AAPB will develop revenue-generating services for digital asset management, including storage, cataloging, and online access for public media outlets across the country. At present, "there isn't enough money in this area," according to Cariani, and so "we are hoping the foundations that helped fund the start of public media sixty plus years ago will want to help conserve those very first programs, but we haven't cracked that door yet."

CONCLUSION

The expansive vision behind AAPB seeks to raise the profile of public media archives. As Cariani puts it, "Any one collection is not nearly as significant or important as all of them together." While still in its early stages, AAPB has demonstrated the rich potential for online access to time-based media archives and the value of large-scale collaborations in managing them.

NOTE

1. Beth Delaney and Annemieke de Jong, "Media Archives and Digital Preservation: Overcoming Cultural Barriers," *New Review of Information and Networking* 20, no. 1–2 (2015): 73–89.

Chapter Six

Cornell University Library Division of Rare and Manuscript Collections

Exploring New Media in the Archive

Peter Botticelli

The Cornell University Library (CUL) Division of Rare and Manuscript Collections (RMC) offers useful insights into how library special collections are adapting to meet the challenge of working with digital information across the life cycle, from the creation of digital assets to online access and long-term preservation. RMC's holdings include a large and varied range of materials, with more than five hundred thousand printed volumes, eighty million manuscripts, and a million other objects, including photographs, paintings, and prints. RMC has collected in such diverse subject areas as East Asia, Iceland, hip-hop, Judaica, and human sexuality, in addition to documenting Cornell and the surrounding community, including archives related to the region's wine industry, for example. RMC is housed in the Carl A. Kroch Library, a facility explicitly designed to foster collaboration by physically uniting CUL's special collections and archives and giving RMC a central, if below-ground-level, location on campus. With the storage space available, RMC's collections have grown significantly in recent decades, including notable acquisitions in the Rose Goldsen Archive of New Media Art and the Human Sexuality Collection, which includes records of organizations such as the National Gay and Lesbian Taskforce and the Human Rights Fund.

INTERVIEWS

In general, we found RMC to be an interesting case given the scope of its collections and its ongoing efforts to develop comprehensive and uniform policies for managing digital assets. We were also interested in how digital assets have fostered collaborations involving librarians, archivists, subject-area curators, and technologists within and outside RMC. To explore these challenges, we conducted in-depth interviews with three people: Anne Sauer, who since 2014 has served as the Stephen E. and Evalyn Edwards Milman Director of RMC; Erin Faulder, who joined RMC as digital archivist in 2016; and Dianne Dietrich, digital projects librarian in the Digital Scholarship and Preservation Services division of CUL.

DIGITAL ASSETS

Taken together, the interviews gave us a clear picture of RMC's long-term needs and objectives as digital assets grow in volume and importance to users. Anne Sauer views RMC as having "amazing collections and mature services" for handling material objects, and yet she acknowledges that the unit has struggled to manage digital assets at scale. Like many institutions, RMC has focused on digital projects organized around the short-term objectives necessitated by grant funding. Sauer hopes to see RMC evolve from a succession of isolated projects to more routine, sustainable digital programs with a longer time horizon, as "projects fall apart, [while] programs go on." Sauer explains that, by necessity, much of RMC's day-to-day work is "executed in a project-based manner," and yet "collecting is more programmatic and focused in particular subject areas with ongoing initiatives," supported in many cases by permanent funding sources. In this context, Sauer sees digital projects as a natural venue for collaboration between curators and technologists, as the expertise of both groups will be necessary to make digital collecting as sustainable as the collecting of material objects. Sauer notes that "curators are focused on building in their collection areas, regardless of format," so with digital objects, it is up to technologists "to figure out how to actually bring them in in a way that is feasible, and that's the part that we've not [yet] done in a systematic way" with an "overarching set of standards or policies and common procedures" guiding the process.

In calling for more extensive collaboration between curators and technologists, Sauer is very much aware of the cultural barriers that exist within library special collections as well as between different library units. Curators are tasked with building collections to support research and teaching in their areas and have tended to operate fairly independently in making acquisition decisions. Increasingly, they find themselves needing to appraise digital materials for acquisition. For digital assets, Sauer clearly sees the need for a more holistic, integrated approach to acquisitions as well as preservation and access—functions that have often been treated as separate from acquisitions in the past. But now "we're seeing the unsustainability of that [model], as materials come in without there being a complete understanding of the implications of acquiring them."

As RMC looks forward to expanding its digital collecting, Sauer is concerned that "we acquire things we can handle or should be able to handle once we get the right systems in place," and so preservation and access concerns need to be taken into account when the decision is made to create or acquire digital objects. To address this need, Sauer envisioned a fundamentally collaborative role for Erin Faulder, enabling her to "understand what the curators' collecting goals are, their visions for the collections," as a first step toward deciding "where the digital part fits" into RMC's larger mission. In this role she would work closely with other staff members to "ensure we have the workflow in place to support those materials when they arrive so that they're stabilized, accessible, and that we're only acquiring things we want to acquire." Sauer notes that these basic issues have always been present for archives, but in general "they're easier to manage with paper than with digital" records. Sauer believes that "for an operation of this size, the only way to manage all this stuff is if everyone who works with the collection is involved. We need it to be the case that the people who are processing collections [of all types] have an understanding of how to handle digital stuff when it comes in," although "with the volume of things coming in, we [also] need collection managers to oversee the workflows and to monitor the big picture." In short, "if you start to do digital stuff and it doesn't change the way your entire day works, then you're not doing it right."

Particularly with born-digital objects, Sauer makes clear, "the people who are acquiring materials need to know what happens when things are processed, and vice versa." The same is true when digital objects are accessed, as "the people facilitating access need to know what happened when the objects were acquired and processed." The larger problem is that "so much of managing born-digital is high touch, with people having a high level of influence on the final product, and the process needs to be more transparent, so everyone has to understand that what they do matters." In essence, for digital assets "we need to know who's the steward" for a given object at each stage of the life cycle, with digital assets clearly understood as a shared, collective responsibility.

To meet the organizational as well as technical challenges of working with digital assets, Sauer emphasizes the need for multidisciplinary teamwork: "What you need is somebody on your team who loves technology, somebody who likes working with collections, somebody who likes working with the public—you need these skills but you don't need to have them all yourself." Sauer believes this is "crucially important" and says, "The biggest gap that we had [when she joined CUL] was having an advocate within RMC to both articulate our needs around digital collections management and help fully shepherd the collaborative process" as it plays out in complex ways across CUL. With material objects, "there's a long and fruitful collaborative tradition between, say, the conservation lab and RMC," as the work of conservators and curators with rare books is "well understood, there's not a lot of mystery about it," and the two groups can work independently even as they coordinate their respective activities. But with born-digital objects, "a more integrated" process is needed to ensure that objects can be adequately preserved and made accessible to users. The job of building integrated, efficient workflows for digital assets is partly an organizational issue, with effective coordination needed across disciplines and areas of specialization, but it's also a distinct technology issue, as the library needs to build (and continually adapt) a digital infrastructure that will adequately serve the needs of its varied constituencies.

One concern for RMC is the relatively small scale of special collections relative to CUL as a whole, making it necessary for RMC to operate within CUL's overall technology ecosystem, even as archives and special collections require specialized workflows for digital objects. Sauer is keenly aware that "digitization has happened here for decades," leading to "massive amounts of digital collections and a massive number of portals, websites, etc., and that's our next knot to untie," as CUL has been moving toward consensus on the need to "migrate digital collections into a more coherent management system." At present, Sauer finds it exciting that "there are people here who can solve these problems, and what I'm trying to do as director is make sure that we have the right people in RMC to go out and actually talk about what we need." In the past, "we've tended to be so busy that there's never been anyone with time to sit down with IT and say, 'What's great about this portal is this, what's not so good is this, it'd be really great if we could have this other thing.'"

This effort builds directly on CUL's relatively long and varied history with digital projects, going back to the 1990s, and the library's experience in managing a number of major transitions in technology over this period. CUL also has recent experience in supporting collaboration through its participation in the Hydra Project, which is building an open source digital repository system. CUL's support for Hydra reflects a long-held desire for a common platform for digital assets, one that might supplant the various systems already in use by CUL, including DSpace, bepress, and the homegrown system long used for ArXiv. RMC itself uses Shared Shelf (an offshoot of Mellon's Artstor, recently renamed as JSTOR/Forum) as an access system, having previously used Luna Imaging software for this purpose. Now it is considering a move to Hydra along with other library units.

TECHNOLOGY PLANNING

RMC has been working actively with other CUL units in making technology plans through a cross-departmental digital assets management committee set up in 2016, which is charged with evaluating how the library's varied systems work together and with making plans for new systems to meet CUL's collection management needs. In managing digitization projects, RMC clearly sees the need for consistent policies on metadata, quality control, and file formats, as opposed to developing policies on a project-by-project basis, a practice that has resulted in substantial variation across projects. For Faulder, it is vital for digitization projects to be informed by "really good practices and standards around capture," and "there's a need to think more holistically from start to finish, from selection to access and even reuse."

These are organizational issues, to be sure, but they have been exacerbated by the lack of an integrated collection management system at RMC, one that would enable the organization to enforce policies governing digital workflows and outputs. One issue is RMC's diverse collections call for a repository system that combines the functionality of collection management systems designed for libraries, archives, and museums. For instance, museum-oriented collection management systems such as TMS (The Museum System) generally support item- or object-level management as opposed to the collection- or series-level management needed for archival records. In providing access to digital assets, Sauer argues, "no CMS right now provides the kind of nuance that we need to manage digital content," including the capacity to "manage access based on restriction types and permissions," with a level of control of sensitive information equivalent to a reading room environment. The choice of access systems is further complicated by the need for RMC to manage objects not just at the item level, as with museum-oriented collection management systems, but also at the collection level, as is routine for archival access systems that focus on the hierarchical relationships within groups of records.

Looking to the future, RMC is keenly aware of the growing demand for more controlled and granular forms of description, going beyond traditional finding aids as well as the MARC-based catalog. CUL's case requires special collections users to navigate through a mix of collection- and item-level records, which in some cases may be mutually exclusive, with item-level records not referencing collections. In the future, RMC hopes to make the discovery process more seamless, integrating the catalog and finding aids and thereby giving users a more direct path from all types of metadata to digital content, including online exhibitions that now tend to be isolated from collection access systems within the institution's web presence. Sauer and Faulder are excited about the potential impact of emerging trends in digital scholarship, as exemplified by the Linked Open Data movement, which calls for users to be given the capacity to discover and view objects through hierarchical as well as nonhierarchical data structures. As Faulder explains, with digital access systems "there is an opportunity to challenge the notion of strict archival arrangement" as users encounter records. Sauer adds, "There's no original order" in digital record keeping, while Faulder argues for a plurality of original orders, with multiple options available to arrange and display records, assuming metadata can be "structured as data not as narrative description." With RMC's large and varied material collections, Sauer views digital humanities scholarship as already a "big driver for digitization work," with the potential to spark much more born-digital collecting in the future.

DONOR EXPECTATIONS

While scholars are clearly demanding improved digital access, RMC has also found rising expectations among donors for digitization and online access to collections, a trend that raises new challenges as well as opportunities for special collections. One example of a recent RMC collecting project with a digital focus involves the archives of entrepreneur Charles Feeny's charitable foundation, Atlantic Philanthropies (AP). Founded in the early 1980s, AP is somewhat unusual in that its founder has long intended to close the foundation (using up its available funds) during his lifetime. Consequently, AP plans to complete all existing grants by 2020. To prepare for the closure, AP agreed to donate its records to RMC, including approximately two thousand cubic feet of paper records and a substantial but as yet unknown volume of born-digital records, including a large volume of email messages. In making the donation, AP put forth ambitious goals regarding access to the records. As Sauer notes, AP did not envision "a typical archives" that might be used by a small number of scholars visiting the repository. Rather, AP wanted to make its archives widely accessible, especially online, with the aim of influencing other philanthropic endeavors similar to the many projects sponsored by AP over the years.

In 2016, RMC began working with AP to draft the donation agreement, a complex process that would end up taking a year to complete. Initially, RMC came up with a "fairly traditional archival project proposal," as Sauer describes it, "with everything in sequence" and focusing on processing and preservation. This did not impress AP, which was determined to have outreach and digitization happening "from the beginning." To address these concerns, RMC organized a six-month project, funded by AP, in which RMC hired a consulting archivist who worked directly with AP staff to appraise the records and to evaluate the potential for digitization and online access, addressing privacy issues, for instance. From Sauer's perspective, acquiring the AP archives was an attractive possibility for RMC, partly because they document the work of a prominent Cornell graduate but more because AP's history of grant making has had a wide and varied impact on many organizations and communities. At the same time, AP has invested substantially in efforts to analyze the impact of its grants, adding much valuable data to the collection. Nonetheless, despite RMC's appraisal of the scholarly value of the collection, Sauer felt compelled to ask if CUL was the right place for the AP archives; of all RMC's acquisitions, Sauer routinely asks, "Does the acquisition support your programmatic mission, not just your collecting mission?" This question has taken on an added importance with the rise of digitization and born-digital collecting, as repositories need to consider not only technology as a factor in appraising and processing collections but the uncertain costs in preserving digital assets for the long term.

DIGITAL PRESERVATION

In fact, digital preservation has been a topic of much interest and concern within RMC as it plans for a future in which digital assets are likely to play a much larger role even as the institution maintains its commitment to preserving material collections. From Sauer's perspective, RMC faces a challenge insofar as "digital preservation has happened somewhere else, not here in RMC" in the past, if only because RMC has been dependent on the rest of CUL for digital infrastructure. Erin Faulder would clearly like preservation management to be a priority within RMC, especially in identifying objects at risk and in setting preservation policies, but, she says, "we have a lot of catch-up to do before we're in a position to start innovating" in this area.

Nonetheless, RMC can draw upon the substantial experience other CUL units have gained in digital preservation. Dianne Dietrich notes that with the prevalence of grant-funded digitization projects over the years, CUL has had a pattern of adopting collection management technologies with access considerations first in mind; yet, once implemented, these systems have become preservation systems by default, as CUL has naturally assumed that digital assets will be maintained permanently, albeit often without explicit plans to do so. Now, according to Dietrich, "there's an active group of us who've said that's not good enough," with efforts underway to develop comprehensive digital preservation plans for the library. One factor supporting this effort is CUL's experience in building a repository service called the Cornell University Library Archival Repository (CULAR), which was designed specifically for preservation rather than access, as it uses a Fedora-based system to manage a dark archive of "low-touch" and relatively well-structured digital objects. CULAR has specialized in bit-level preservation, with tools to ensure the fixity of digital objects but lacking the advanced services, such as format migration and emulation, that may be needed to preserve digital objects in the long run.

By focusing on bit preservation, CULAR was able to achieve scale in a relatively short amount of time. But now, for Faulder and Dietrich, the main challenge facing preservation repositories is to be not just scalable but also sufficiently flexible in supporting curators as they go about managing preservation risks for diverse object types. Ideally, RMC would like a repository system that required a minimum of customization from one collection or project to another, by enforcing clear, granular policies for data interoperability, and adequately supported access needs as well as preservation. Above all, RMC wants to move away from the default pattern of storing digital assets on local servers and adopting access systems to meet short-term needs, as exemplified by RMC's ongoing use of Shared Shelf to store the output of digitization projects in advance of developing preservation plans.

In general, Faulder and Dietrich agree that digital preservation is not yet a mature service within CUL, although critical steps have been taken toward making it a routine function. For her part, Sauer notes, "Our management of born-digital collections has been minimal up to this point," especially before Faulder's hiring as the first person at RMC with a focus on born-digital assets. One practical issue RMC faces with born-digital assets stems from the fact that it has been inadvertently collecting digital records in the form of thousands of storage discs representing a variety of media types (DVD, CD, Zip, etc.) and file formats. The discs typically arrive at RMC attached to or embedded in paper files and are only discovered as the physical materials are processed, complicating RMC's archival workflow. Much of this data is clearly at risk, and RMC staff acknowledge the need to identify and describe the files as soon as possible and to capture their contents using preservation-worthy storage media and file formats. But RMC still has a significant backlog in processing these materials, especially as substantial human intervention is often needed to identify the contents of individual files, determine how they relate to paper records, and decide how best to prevent the risk of data loss through technology obsolescence.

DIGITAL COLLECTING

A good example of how digital age collecting at RMC has complicated preservation is the Rose Goldsen Archive of New Media Art, a repository of new media art and resources with an ambitious agenda of supporting digital scholarship and creative activity. The Goldsen collection began with a 2002 symposium titled "Art of CD-ROM," which led RMC to acquire multimedia collage works created using proprietary applications such as Macromedia Director and stored on CD-ROM discs, a format popular in the 1990s due to its low cost and relatively high storage capacity compared to other media commonly in use at the time, including hard drives. The contents of the CD-ROMs depend on a variety of obsolete technologies, including operating systems, application software, and hardware. As CD-ROM–based artworks are an obsolete yet relatively new genre, describing their content and technical characteristics (e.g., file formats), as well as the access requirements for the collection objects, requires substantial effort. But identifying and characterizing the objects is only the first step. Of greater concern is the effort that will be needed to mitigate the current and future obsolescence risks facing the collection.

To explore these issues, CUL received a National Endowment for the Humanities grant in 2013 for the Preservation and Access Frameworks for Digital Art Objects (PAFDAO) Project, which focused on emulation as a basic preservation technique for the Goldsen collection. As Dianne Dietrich notes, emulation may prove an important means to preserve digital artworks if it is necessary "to preserve the environment" around the objects, including web browsers and operating systems. The PAFDAO team used a sample of roughly one hundred CD-ROMs as a testbed of objects dating mainly from 1998 to 2000. The discs were imaged and described, and the content was tested, revealing some extant data losses owing to media degradation. Next, the project tested software emulators for a sampling of the CD-ROMs. In carrying out this task, PAFDAO had to work around the fact that software developers, including those in the digital forensics market, have limited incentives to maintain backward compatibility with older operating systems, making it necessary to preserve old computing equipment—an expensive and technically difficult proposition—or to use emulation to make objects usable with current technology as it evolves over time.

In seeking to emulate the test objects, the PAFDAO team was able to identify Macintosh emulators maintained by the enthusiast community for versions of the operating system dating to before the release of OS X in 2001, marking the biggest single transition in the history of the Macintosh platform since it was introduced in 1984. For RMC, the experience with emulators afforded by PAFDAO exposed a number of issues that will require ongoing attention. One problem is the need to maintain and update emulation software, especially in the absence of commercial investment and for proprietary systems with complex licensing issues. A second problem is directly curatorial; while the team was able to find emulators that work well at a technical level, they found instances in which changes in hardware make objects look different from the user's perspective. Images that were originally rendered using 1990s-era CRT monitors may look different with current LCD technologies. For interactive objects, the faster processor speeds and input devices (e.g., using a trackpad versus a mouse) in up-to-date computers may alter or distort the user's experience—for instance, with on-screen behaviors happening faster than was originally intended. The results of PAFDAO gave RMC valuable insights into the archival implications of actions that might be taken to preserve digital objects. The project showed how the value of authenticity might be impacted by a technique such as emulation, one that can provide a reasonable approximation, though not an exact representation, of an object as it appeared to the creator.

RESEARCH LIBRARY VERSUS MUSEUM APPROACHES

Given the uncertain and varying outcomes of digital preservation actions, RMC is cognizant of how the decisions made by a research library might differ from those made by a museum. The former might approach preservation more from an archival perspective, treating objects as records of past activity and documenting technology as it existed at the time of creation. By contrast, a museum might be more aggressive in adapting objects to new technologies in an effort to preserve the underlying aesthetic or experiential values the creator had in mind, especially in cases where an artist has not provided clear specifications for the technologies employed to display or use an object. In any case, Faulder believes that in carrying out digital preservation, information professionals "make choices that have a far greater effect on the content we preserve than with physical material." For archivists in particular, "the reality is that there is an enormous amount of labor involved in processing digital records, and we need to be transparent" about actions taken to preserve and provide access to digital records. Faulder also sees digital preservation as having a direct impact on the work of records appraisal, with decisions about which objects to retain and in what form becoming more of a shared responsibility between archivists and technology specialists, reflecting the need to develop reliable metrics to evaluate the technology-related costs involved in storing and preserving digital assets on a permanent basis.

Sauer believes that libraries, archives, and museums (LAMs) have made progress recently in building their capacity to manage technology, particularly through their experience in migrating data from old systems to new ones. Sauer readily acknowledges that digital asset management in general is "not all figured out yet," especially given the natural tendency to focus on the "shiny new tool" rather than seeking to manage the whole technology ecosystem. Sauer is a keen advocate for planning "exit strategies" for technologies in use, giving the institution long-range plans to guide the study and adoption of new systems as they become available. Also, for digital objects Sauer has embraced a "create once" philosophy, in which LAMs actively seek to minimize potential disruptions to digital objects by carefully organizing and describing content at a granular level, with the aim of creating self-contained, portable digital objects that will ideally be reusable in a variety of repository systems.

FUTURE EFFORTS

Taken as a whole, our interviews showed RMC to be at a transition point, as the organization continues to move from a focus on digitization projects and early-stage preservation efforts like PAFDAO toward more uniform and routine preservation and access services and policies. In the near term, Faulder sees the growth of digitized assets still outpacing the acquisition of born-digital content; yet the latter is likely to grow dramatically over time, and libraries are all but certain to find born-digital collections to be "significantly more diverse in formats and in how collections are used" compared to recent experience with digital surrogates representing material collections. To cope with the flood of born-digital content, with the accompanying technical and organizational challenges, RMC believes substantial new investments will be needed to upgrade the library's infrastructure, and continuing research and education will be needed to inform CUL's work with digital assets as the digital environment continues to evolve. For Erin Faulder, the "solution is being able to treat digital content not as projects but as a program that requires support, active management, and that requires resources. It's a commitment issue." Sauer agrees, emphasizing the need for advocacy by collecting units such as RMC as they adapt to digital needs while maintaining their commitment to existing material collections. Most importantly, Sauer regularly finds herself "encouraging the staff here to feel like they can be vocal" in articulating their technology needs, as "it's up to us to say what we need"; "it's our job" to speak up and to avoid negative assumptions about what is possible—claiming, for instance, "I don't think IT's going to do that" rather than putting forth a positive vision for which technology might be the best option for the library. Faulder concurs, seeing her role as essentially providing a resource for RMC, including training and advocacy as well as hands-on work with digital collections. Sauer herself views advocacy as a critical feature of her role as director: "I feel like that's the sum total of my job, to advocate for the people here . . . talking to donors, working with library leadership to explain what we need," and above all making the case for RMC as "a good investment" for CUL.

CONCLUSION

We found that for RMC, digital asset management is fundamentally a high-touch activity, with day-to-day decisions seen as having a potentially large impact on the long-term value and meaning of digital collections. RMC views planning as a vitally important function for the library, perhaps even more so than the technical aspects of working with digital objects. Most importantly, planning for digital access and preservation depends very much on collaboration, as the resource-intensive nature of digital assets requires the organization to design complex workflows, to carefully evaluate new technologies as they emerge, and to make sound decisions about which technologies to adopt. For a collecting unit such as RMC, key decisions affecting digital assets cannot be made in isolation from other library units, especially as collaboration is needed to bring together all the varied expertise needed to ensure that digital collections are effectively preserved and made accessible to users.

Chapter Seven

The Museum of Modern Art

A Cross-Institutional Collaboration

Peter Botticelli

The Museum of Modern Art (MoMA) is an important example of a museum with a mission to document living artists and movements in contemporary art. Since it was founded in 1929, MoMA has managed to assemble one of the world's premier collections of twentieth-century art. In keeping with its mission, MoMA's library special collections and institutional archives provide critical documentation on twentieth-century art. This case looks at the unusually successful collaboration achieved across curatorial and library/archives boundaries.

INTERVIEWS

To explore MoMA's approach to library and archival collections, we interviewed Milan Hughston, chief of library (he retired from this position in 2017), and Michelle Elligott, chief of archives. In studying MoMA, our initial aim was to understand how museum libraries and archives have pursued digitization and online access. Our interviews did reveal much about the impact of technology at MoMA; yet we also heard a broader story of a museum library that has been successful in raising its institutional visibility by consolidating collections, widening its collecting policy, and reorganizing itself to highlight the different yet complementary roles of library and archival collections.

HISTORY OF MoMA

Milan Hughston joined MoMA in 2000 as chief of library and museum archives. Previously, he had been a librarian at the Amon Carter Museum of American Art, where he was responsible for establishing the museum's archives program. Hughston arrived at MoMA with a mandate to consolidate library services, including a number of library resources that had previously been distributed across the museum's curatorial departments. In reflecting on this effort, Hughston points to the fact that MoMA's curatorial departments were "relatively small" by comparison with departments in larger museums with encyclopedic collecting policies, in which curators are often able to maintain a substantial degree of independence within their respective collecting areas. By contrast, MoMA has been able to sustain a relatively high degree of collaboration across departmental boundaries, enabling the library and archives to work closely with curators, administrators, and donors. Hughston himself credits MoMA's relatively narrow collecting focus as a key factor in promoting a culture of collaboration among curators, librarians, and archivists. As a point of comparison, he cites the Amon Carter Museum, his former employer, as an institution that specializes in American art and photography up to the mid-twentieth century; Hughston says, "How lucky I've been to work for museums with a focused collection policy; this has made it much easier to know how to build the collection and to promote it."

Beyond the effort to consolidate library resources, Hughston's early years at MoMA were dominated by a major building project from 2002 to 2006, a process that disrupted day-to-day operations across the whole museum while MoMA's Manhattan footprint was dramatically enlarged and reshaped. Along with the curatorial departments, the library and archival collections were moved to MoMA QNS, a large storage facility in Queens that was open to researchers one day a week. Upon completion of the building project in 2006, the library and archives moved into the new Lewis B. and Dorothy Cullman Education and Research Building in Manhattan, which gave it an efficient, attractive, and centrally located facility overlooking MoMA's landmark courtyard. In managing the building project, Hughston prioritized strategic planning for his department, as it was clear that near-term decisions regarding the new facilities would have a long-term impact on the value of MoMA's library and archival collections.

One key issue was how best to allocate storage space between the new Manhattan building (once it was completed) and MoMA QNS, which the museum planned to continue using as a storage space after curatorial operations moved back to Manhattan. As Hughston recalls, "We knew there would never be enough space in Manhattan for the entire collection." Indeed, the four years of the building project marked the only time when all library and archives collections resided under a single roof. Moreover, the space afforded by MoMA QNS gave the library and archives a welcome opportunity to acquire additional archives that had been accumulated by curatorial departments over the years. Acting strategically, the library and archives was able to take advantage of the disruption caused by the building project by helping curators solve the problem of managing archival materials that existed outside the art collection. Seeing the value of an expanded and centralized museum archives, Hughston made a point of including the archives as part of the capital campaign for the new building, a move supported by senior curators and administrators that afforded the archives its first dedicated space for researchers.

This was an important step forward, especially as the MoMA Archives was formally established only in 1989, whereas the MoMA Library was founded in 1932. In the absence of a formal archival program, MoMA had accumulated business records and curatorial documentation organically, as exemplified by the personal records of MoMA's founding director, Alfred Barr, which scholars have used regularly in examining the history of twentieth-century art as well as the museum itself. Initially, according to Hughston, the archives' "primary mission, like most museum archives, was to preserve and collect enduring records of the institution," and much of its work was taken up with processing the sixty-year backlog of records and updating finding aids to current standards.

Yet, by the late 1990s, the library and archives had begun to collect records from outside MoMA, under a broadened collecting policy that aimed to document the artists represented in the museum's permanent collection and exhibitions. In explaining this policy shift, Hughston observes that "it's hard to tell the story of modern contemporary art without using archival material, special collections, and ephemera," such as artists' books. Still, MoMA made a conscious decision not to compete with the Archives of American Art or other institutions that actively pursue artists' personal records. Instead, the library and archives "decided that we could be selective about expanding the scope of the archives so we wouldn't have to turn away records that really help tell the story of modern contemporary art." This was a departure from the historic pattern in which the library and archives had been "fairly reactive to the museum's curatorial policies both in acquisitions and exhibition programming," in Hughston's words. In practice, however, "we've been able to be a little more proactive in collecting special collections materials because we're not considered a curatorial department, which means we operate under a different set of rules" that afford greater flexibility—an advantage that led one curator to advise Hughston, "Don't ever change that!"

EXPANDING THE ARCHIVES

Since widening the collecting policy, the library and archives has been able to make a number of valuable acquisitions that directly complement the museum's curatorial work. One recent example consists of archives documenting the 1960s Fluxus movement; this "filled a gap in the Museum's collecting for that period," according to Hughston, with the help of a prominent collector and donor. Such acquisitions, along with the increased visibility of the library and archives after the return to Manhattan in 2006, have led to a dramatic increase in usage for library special collections and archives, including a strong demand for loans to other museums. In fact, as much as a third of the museum's total loans to other institutions in recent years have involved archives. MoMA has also seen a large increase in the use of archives in public exhibitions. In explaining the growing interest in archives, Michelle Elligott points to recent trends in the arts and humanities that give primary source materials a renewed prominence as well as new uses, especially as digital technologies have afforded new ways to view and interpret material objects. Elligott has witnessed this trend firsthand, having joined MoMA in 1999 with a background in both art history and archives management, a combination she has found useful in engaging scholars and artists as they continue to rethink the boundaries between records and art objects. During a recent program giving artists a quiet time in the museum galleries after regular visiting hours, Elligott made a point of opening the archives during the event. To her surprise, as many as a hundred artists chose to visit the reading room.

With the rising prominence of archival materials, in 2014 the library and archives decided to split into separate departments, with Michelle Elligott serving as chief of archives and Hughston as chief of library. Given the small number of permanent staff and the physical proximity of both units in the Cullman Building, it was assumed that the library and archives would continue to work together closely as equal partners in managing special collections and archives at MoMA. For Hughston and Elligott, the move was intended to maintain the library's central role in curatorial work while further raising the visibility of the archives. A key goal was to boost fund-raising efforts to support each unit, including work with dedicated interest groups within the wider Friends of MoMA. In the long run, Hughston and Elligott hope that the split will lead to more full-time staff for both units as they carve out more distinct roles within the museum. For Elligott, it was particularly important to highlight the archives' role in records management and, by extension, institutional governance at MoMA, especially with the demands imposed by MoMA's fast-growing body of electronic records, for which the archives has completed a two-year test project that Elligott hopes will lead MoMA to build a full-fledged digital repository.

COLLABORATION WITH NYARC

Ultimately, Hughston and Elligott see collaboration across departmental as well as institutional lines as the best way forward for libraries, archives, and museums. Hughston points to the New York Art Resources Consortium (NYARC), founded in 2006, as a prime example of collaboration among art museum libraries. In his view, "Museums have tended to be lone wolves, whereas libraries have tended to be more open to cooperative ventures." At the same time, librarians have long been perceived as "thought leaders in technology," as in many museums "it was the library that had the first integrated, automated system" for managing collection information. By promoting NYARC as a library-led initiative, Hughston was able to build support within MoMA for the consortium as a logical means to "move forward together in ways we couldn't do individually" with the resource and technology constraints facing MoMA and the other members. As a multi-institutional collaboration, NYARC has been able to attract significant foundation support for improved access systems and to initiate a web archiving service.

COLLABORATION WITHIN MOMA

Beyond its participation in external collaborations such as NYARC, MoMA has recently worked to build up its own digital capacity and to foster collaboration across departments holding digital assets. In the pursuit of these goals, an important step was taken in 2014 with the hiring of Fiona Romeo to the newly created position of director of digital content and strategy. Hughston observes, "We frankly needed someone with that role, a senior position that would bring together the various data silos and revamp the institution's web presence." From his experience as a museum librarian, Hughston observes that while librarians have always been concerned with making knowledge accessible, museums have tended to own collection data that have been "lovingly created but not with an idea on how to share them with the general public." While the library and archives units have been strongly committed to digitization and online access, Hughston acknowledges that neither the existing library and archives staff nor the MoMA IT department could fill the collaborative role envisioned for Romeo, whose first major initiative would be MoMA's groundbreaking exhibition history project, which went online in 2016 with a web page dedicated to each of MoMA's exhibitions since the museum opened in 1929.

This project aimed to document MoMA's exhibition history by combining digitized press releases, checklists, approximately thirty thousand installation photographs, and the full text of catalogs. For Michelle Elligott, the online exhibition history represents the culmination of two decades of archival work at MoMA, including efforts to consolidate, process, and digitize archival records and to encode finding aids, which are linked to the exhibition web pages. Elligott also sees the exhibition history project as paving the way for a similar effort to digitize the MoMA PS1 exhibition records and to advance efforts to digitize other archives and special collections at MoMA, such as the Alfred Barr papers. The exhibitions project also coincided with an effort to upgrade and expand access to the Museum Archives Image Database, which contains roughly forty thousand digitized images. In the long run, Elligott sees the further integration of primary source materials across MoMA as a critical goal in furthering the museum's mission for the digital age. Indeed, in 2017, following Hughston's retirement, Elligott was named chief of archives, library, and research collections. Over the last fifteen years MoMA has laid the foundation for further collaboration across departments.

CONCLUSION

MoMA has been a successful venue for cross-disciplinary collaboration in recent years, thanks in large part to decisions made by the museum's leadership. Yet, in hindsight, it's worth considering how the institution's underlying mission may have paved the way for effective collaboration in the long run. As a museum dedicated to collecting and interpreting culture as it is being created, MoMA has had an unusual opportunity to document the creative process in greater detail than has often been possible for museums collecting antiquities. At the same time, our understanding of twentieth-century art has been shaped to an unusual extent by the presence of documentation that lies beyond the object itself. Scholars today want to know in detail why and how a collection like MoMA's was assembled, just as many artists in the age of mass media came to expect their audiences to have prior knowledge of the people or ideas depicted on canvas or paper. For instance, to understand Andy Warhol's work, we need to understand the peculiar cultural dynamic he exploited, in which the very ubiquity of a mass-produced soup can (as with his many images of celebrities) would add value to his paintings rather than detract from them. In this context, it makes sense that MoMA's library and archival collections would play a more prominent, central role than might be the case for other museums where objects can, or must, stand on their own before the viewer. As with its pioneering efforts to collect twentieth-century art, MoMA's recent digital efforts suggest a move toward greater convergence—blurring the boundaries between library, archives, and museum—as the museum positions itself to remain a leading repository for contemporary culture.

Chapter Eight

The Boston Public Library

An Effective Strategy for Advancing Digital Access

Peter Botticelli

The Boston Public Library (BPL) was opened to the public in 1854, and since then it has accumulated a number of historic "firsts" in the American public library movement.[1] Through the donation of a number of important research collections, the institution quickly evolved into a major research library as well as a lending institution. BPL now has a circulating collection of roughly 1.2 million volumes and a research collection with over 22 million items, including rare books, manuscripts, archives, maps, prints, sound recordings, and photographs. BPL's experience over the past decade has made the library a valuable case example of collaboration as a means to advance digitization and online access.

INTERVIEWS

To understand BPL's approach to digital assets, we interviewed three people who have played leading roles in shaping BPL's digital strategy.[2] As manager of digital projects and more recently as manager of content discovery, Tom Blake has played a key role in starting up and managing digitization projects since he joined BPL in 2005, after having worked on digitization projects at the Massachusetts Historical Society. Danny Pucci, as lead digital projects librarian, has overseen metadata creation for digital projects since 2008. Finally, we interviewed David Leonard, who joined BPL as chief technology officer in 2009 and is now president.

DIGITIZATION

BPL saw its early digitization efforts as experiments or small-scale pilot projects that aimed primarily to give the library experience with the new technology. As Leonard observes, after a decade's experience, the digitization is "now much more strategic," and the library has become "more deliberative" in selecting items to digitize as its digital workflows have matured. Leonard notes that with the pace of digitization "still increasing" in scale, BPL today "has its arms around the special collections area in a much more interesting way than it did ten years ago." He attributes this to the fact that "as the skills of people in curatorial positions have evolved, we're now better prepared to make commitments and decisions about what should come online next." In the early days, with so many items available to digitize, it was a matter of saying, "We'll do a few of these, or this little collection here and there," whereas today the library needs to "make informed decisions about how to set priorities, because you can't take a collection of twenty-three million objects and expect to digitize everything, or that everything is digitizable"—there may, for instance, be copyright restrictions or an object might duplicate other online resources such as government publications. Still, BPL's long-term goal is to have "the vast majority of special collections fully online, as a whole special collection."

Since 2005, when the library's digitization efforts were jump-started with an Institute of Museum and Library Services grant, BPL has actively looked for ways to scale up its digital capacity. In the early days, the digital services team "learned as they went, starting with spreadsheets and file systems," according to Leonard, "and it was really only after 2009 that we managed to build our first digital repository system." Before that, "there had been pilots and attempts which were fine on a limited basis but that weren't really scalable or sustainable." Nevertheless, BPL was able to take a big step forward in 2007, when it partnered with the Internet Archive (IA) and agreed to host one of IA's regional scanning centers, with advanced equipment and methods for handling bound volumes. IA's equipment complemented BPL's own photography lab, which was better equipped to scan the library's large print and photograph collections. With IA's support, by 2017 thousands of BPL's rare books had been scanned and made available through IA's own site. With the success of this partnership, BPL recently agreed to transfer ownership of approximately two hundred thousand LP and 78 rpm records to IA. For Leonard, this move will "facilitate better storage, preservation, digitization, and where copyright allows, online access through the IA site with credit to the BPL." Such an agreement "required a level of trust between BPL and IA which our early history shored up, and it also required some evolutionary thinking on how society wants to make our historical records online." Regarding preservation, the fact remains that "vinyl decays, so these are materials that would ultimately be lost without a project such as this." While BPL and IA are very different institutions with different histories, David Leonard sees an important parallel, as "the public library and BPL in particular was a bold, creative, crazy idea in 1848, so there's a piece of what the IA is doing for the twenty-first century that is equally as bold, creative, and crazy in the digital world."

FLICKR

Beyond the resources provided by IA, BPL looked for other external support for putting its digitized special collections online. In 2008, BPL followed the example of a number of libraries, archives, and museums (LAMs), including the Library of Congress, in launching a Flickr site, which BPL saw as a low-cost way to raise the library's visibility online.[3] Tom Blake also saw Flickr as a viable source of user data, particularly as BPL found that images on Flickr tended to rank higher in search results than those published on BPL's own website, thereby helping Blake answer a big strategic question: "What is the point of the digitization lab?" Like other institutions, BPL embraced the idea that audiences were increasingly apt to discover content through social media rather than institutional websites, with the implication that LAMs should "work to move their content from single access point portals to larger shared spaces."[4] Yet BPL found some clear limitations to Flickr, particularly regarding metadata. Using Flickr's single "description" field, BPL found ways to "fake out the Flickr database to make structured data as best we could," using basic HTML tags, according to Danny Pucci. Another technical issue was the need to upload and tag images by hand, which limited BPL to uploading about one hundred images per week at first, a figure that grew to several hundred per week once the team learned to use open source tools to speed the upload process.

By 2015, BPL had managed to upload a total of nearly one hundred thousand images to Flickr, including prints, posters, photographs, postcards, murals, cartoons, trading cards, broadsides, drawings, and ephemera. Exposing these materials in Flickr gave the BPL a number of useful lessons. One is the potential value of online comments posted to Flickr. For instance, a commenter identified an image of jazz musician Paul Whiteman, enabling BPL to update its own metadata. Another lesson is the importance of search engine optimization. In a search for "Leslie Jones photographer," for example, BPL's Flickr image came up as the third result after the artist's own website and Wikipedia page. Flickr also highlighted the need for a practical means to display multipart objects, as Flickr treats images as separate items, leaving the description field as the only way to directly link a series of images.

DIGITAL COMMONWEALTH

While Flickr provided a quick way for BPL to provide online access to digital images, from the outset the digital services team clearly understood its limitations as they went about the task of planning for a full-scale digital asset management (DAM) system that would eventually meet all of BPL's needs for storage, processing, and access to the institution's rapidly growing volume of digital assets. For BPL, a key decision point came in 2011, when the library decided to hire two software developers to build a customized DAM system with open source technology. This objective coincided with BPL being named Library for the Commonwealth, thereby extending BPL's services to all Massachusetts residents. With this broadened mandate, BPL became the logical home for the Digital Commonwealth (DC), a consortium of Massachusetts LAMs founded in 2007, which initially did not count BPL among its members. The new partnership between BPL and DC, formalized in 2011, was supported initially with a $100,000 Library Services and Technology Act grant for a feasibility study; in 2012, $2.2 million in state funds were allocated to enable BPL to begin offering free digitization services to cultural heritage institutions across the state and to host the DC repository. Once these services were established, DC received a permanent line on the state budget. With this stable funding source in place, Leonard sees the BPL-DC partnership as marking an important "evolution from the print world to the twenty-first-century digital world." BPL has gone from library of last recourse—where patrons could go if a book was not available at their local libraries—to the Library for the Commonwealth, in which BPL plays an active role for patrons across the state.

For Massachusetts LAMs, the offer of free (or fully state-funded) digitization services through DC naturally led to a backlog of digitization projects and a rapid rate of growth in the items made available through the DC portal, which went online as a beta site in August 2013. By 2015, when DC was launched formally, it already contained almost two hundred thousand images drawn from over 120 institutions. As of 2017, this number had risen past four hundred thousand. With the rise of DC, the Digital Services Department has become an important facet of BPL's outreach efforts as the Library for the Commonwealth. When a LAM makes a request for digitization, a BPL staff member will conduct a site visit to evaluate materials as candidates for digitization, taking both access and preservation needs into consideration. BPL also employs a statewide metadata coordinator who advises institutions on how to create metadata in line with DC's standards.

In understanding how DC works in practice, Leonard points out the "need to distinguish between DC the project and DC the organization," which operate "hand in hand but which are invisible" to those on the outside. As a project, "BPL is actually the agent doing it, which is helping institutions across the state get their materials online." Hence, DC is "a project of the BPL; it's the library's repository, but it also serves as the statewide repository for partner organizations." As a collaboration, the DC membership has to place a substantial degree of trust in BPL to manage the technology and workflows needed to support a repository at this level of scale and complexity. David Leonard believes that "the longer-term members see value in continuing to work together, to collaborate—that's what's gotten institutionalized" in DC, beyond the project-related work involved in digitizing collections and in building and refining the repository infrastructure. Leonard sees a progression. "In the early stages, for many who just started out it was a project; 'I want to get my yearbooks online, my glass negatives online.'" In working toward finite, short-term goals such as these, LAMs naturally tended to welcome the state funding and technical support provided through BPL. Yet, in the longer-term view, DC has always faced a challenge in convincing LAMs that it makes sense to use a statewide portal as the primary vehicle for providing access to digitized collections. It was important that DC "made it a requirement that if we're helping you bring your collection online, then it has to be shareable through this network," even as LAMs are still able to build their own repositories. Open access was mandated explicitly by the state in its decision to fund DC. But the idea of repositories as large-scale aggregators was also inherent in the technology and in the desire of users to discover resources across repositories and institutional boundaries. As DC has grown, Leonard believes, "we've all evolved together, BPL and DC as a membership organization, towards an understanding that digital services, the way of providing access to our various communities, involves digital being part and parcel of who we are and what we do."

DIGITAL PUBLIC LIBRARY OF AMERICA

As a digital collaboration, the close partnership between BPL and DC took a step forward in 2013, when DC joined the Digital Public Library of America (DPLA), which is now physically housed at BPL's main site at Copley Square in Boston. DC became a DPLA Service Hub, in which the DC members' collections are aggregated at the national level through DPLA's interface as well as at the state level through DC's own access system. From the perspective of BPL, DPLA represents a strategic opportunity for LAMs to serve users in new and better ways, but as a collaborative undertaking, it will require LAMs to share resources and build consensus in deciding how a shared digital repository should operate. David Leonard sees DPLA today as coming to an inflection point, as it decides "what it should do now that it's exiting what is effectively its pilot stage." Leonard clearly views DPLA as a successful pilot project: "We've proven the value of DPLA, but now what is the right role for a national digital public library, and how do we make that sustainable?"

For BPL in particular, digitization has led to a big strategic issue concerning the optimal design of the library's digital repository infrastructure. In this regard, DPLA represents a distinct model for building a shared, distributed infrastructure around the service and content hubs that are at the core of DPLA's technology strategy. In essence, the DPLA partnership calls for "50-plus service hubs that will deal with whatever local concerns there are on the technology front," according to Leonard. Once these local or regional centers are in place and providing adequate services to individual LAMs, DPLA can focus on "harvesting the metadata of the content and service hubs, which makes it more scalable than pretending this is a giant repository." By contrast, Leonard sees IA's technology strategy as "collecting the objects themselves," as opposed to just metadata, and "putting them in multiple places as a way of dealing with not just scalability but also preservation." For Leonard, it's still an open question as to which architecture, or which combination of technical approaches, will provide optimum value for institutions such as BPL and the DC membership. At least, recent experience has given the community "some interesting models to look at," he says, "and I think the next five to ten years will be very interesting in terms of how all of us together will determine what is next."

To form and maintain effective collaborations in building the technology infrastructure, it will be necessary for LAMs to start with the strategy conversation about how institutions can best serve users with their available resources. In essence, LAMs will need to work through a complex set of organizational as well as technology issues in deciding how partnerships like DC and DPLA should proceed. For Leonard, DPLA in particular raises an essential question: "Is this the Library of Congress online, [but] with a distributed model, or is this a public library aggregator, or is this some sort of membership organization to which you pay fees and then get a service? And there may be multiple answers to these questions."

BPL itself has embraced collaboration in building its digital infrastructure, and so far it has been successful in aligning its own strategy for digital access with the models adopted by DC and DPLA on one side and IA on the other. Ultimately, BPL has adopted the view that optimizing discovery and access may require the library to make collection objects available through shared repository systems. Tom Blake, for one, sees no conflict in having digital collections residing in more than one place online, and he actually expresses a wariness of portals becoming too centralized, potentially leading to a "resiloing" of collections that should be more accessible digitally than in physical form.

CONVERGENCE IN PRACTICE

With its general commitment to the vision of a shared or distributed digital repository, BPL has embraced the idea of convergence in the LAM sector with varied types of collection objects made accessible through a common repository platform. As Leonard notes in the case of BPL, "We're an 'L,' an 'A,' and an 'M,' in many ways," with the result that the library's digital strategy needs to take all three major collection types into consideration. For Leonard, the potential value of convergence for online users "wasn't necessarily true or understood five years ago." The problem was that LAMs were unsure of how to strike a balance in their resource commitments to physical as opposed to digital collections. "I think we feared that the digital would replace the in-person, whereas I think now our more mature understanding of our reality is that it is somehow a blend of both, and the exact blend is what is yet to be worked out." Leonard poses three fundamental questions for LAMs to answer as they build digital repositories. First, "how do we support interesting use cases as things come online?" In education, for instance, can technology enable LAMs to play a more effective and immersive role in the classroom? Second, Leonard is convinced that "there are opportunities to make the reading experience even richer" with technology by augmenting text with various interactive technologies. So far, "we've done user-generated content, but what's beyond that?" Third, from the public library perspective, Leonard is concerned with how technology may affect the in-person experience of using the library. "When I come to the physical library, how does the technology get used to enrich my experience, or do I use technology in an innovative way that I couldn't do otherwise?"

Broadly speaking, Leonard believes that as digitized collections continue to grow, "the challenge for the next phase or next iteration of this work is around use, and not just in making objects available online," so "are there curated experiences either done by the library staff or that are facilitated for the end users to do for themselves?" As a case example, Leonard points to BPL's Norman B. Leventhal Map Center, which is working actively to teach K–12 teachers how to better use maps in the classroom; Leonard sees the center's collection as a model for maximizing the impact of many types of special collections as they become available online.

In general, BPL views adaptation as a key factor in shaping its online presence as user needs continue to evolve over time. At present, Leonard sees three interesting use cases operating at different levels. First, at a very basic level, public libraries, including BPL, would like to support users in sharing pictures of general interest, particularly through social media. Second, at a more advanced level, the library would like to help users make serendipitous connections between online resources, "such as looking at a map of your town or your street from a hundred years ago and making some connection about local history or family history." Such connections "may be very valuable but perhaps aren't scalable" for the library. Third, as a research library, BPL sees much value in making scholarly resources more visible and accessible online. For example, through an online search of BPL's rare books collection, a scholar was able to identify a play as having been written by a contemporary of Shakespeare.

To support such varied use cases, Leonard believes the way forward for BPL is to think beyond the boundaries of the institutional website and instead to "think about the online connected presence of the BPL," which includes the website plus social media, mobile apps, and so forth—wherever BPL's content might appear online. Leonard believes that LAMs are now placing a greater value on their online presence than before. "Five to ten years ago people would have thought of that as 'that's just about marketing, that's just about messaging, that's just about getting your information out there,'" whereas today LAM administrators are increasingly "driven by a focus on customer service, the user experience," regardless of whether this takes place online or in person. In the online environment, LAMs are increasingly asking themselves how to achieve "a level of interactivity that makes sense so that you actually can have an impact on someone's life or information need in the same way the physical library does and has done in the past." For Leonard, this marks a shift in thinking about the institutional website, moving beyond the earlier view that the web is for "presenting information, describing programs, describing collections" as opposed to creating immersive experiences that could match the value of in-person visits.

A key example of an immersive digital experience for public libraries involves e-books. In 2015, BPL first reached a million e-book downloads, and the demand has continued to rise since then, even as the rate of decline for print appears to be slowing, or perhaps reaching a plateau, according to Leonard, who sees the need for libraries to strike an appropriate "balance between a level of use and consumption of e-books and print material," with the understanding that in the future some users may insist on reading only print materials, while others may read only e-books, and others may prefer a mix of both. In any case, Leonard believes that e-books "won't ever fully replace the role of printed materials, but I don't know that we're at the right balance" today. In part, it's a problem of the availability of e-books, which in the past has been limited by commercial and copyright dilemmas facing publishers and libraries. But it's also a usability issue and ultimately a content issue for Leonard. In the past, "a book used to be a three-dimensional object with pages and pictures, and, yes, you can have that online" by simulating a print book through formats like PDF or ePub. But then, why not think more broadly about the potential of e-books and envision "a rich experience that is multimedia or audiovisually enabled in a way that you could not do before?" However, in designing (or at least helping to design) such experiences, librarians will need to consider a fundamental question: "What does that mean for reading?" Ultimately, to utilize digital technology to the fullest, "the LAM profession will need to understand reading and literacy skills at a much deeper level," with a more explicit knowledge of cognitive development and early literacy skills. At the same time, librarians need to "understand the economics and the business models involved in not just publishing but the broader technology industry," and LAMs need to develop the capacity to shape the experience afforded by e-books and by the different experience of using "digital objects in a DAM system" or as they might be published on an institutional website.

ORGANIZATIONAL MODEL

In a rapidly evolving technology environment, the question of how to foster and sustain innovation has been and will continue to be an important issue for LAMs. In the mid-2000s, as BPL took its initial steps in digitization and digital asset management, an organizational model was needed that would enable digital projects to thrive within the hierarchical, compartmentalized structure that had long characterized BPL and other large public libraries. Leonard notes that "organizations today tend to be more collaborative and with flatter structures, and we're certainly moving in that direction, but for a 170-year-old organization that's part of a municipal government, there's only so fast you can go." In the early days, BPL opted to set up "dedicated teams and departments that were just doing digital" and had much freedom to innovate. This strategy was a success, but Leonard is quick to note that "ten years on from some of those early initiatives, we're seeing that digital work is much more integrated" across the library as a whole. In the area of technical services, for instance, the handling of physical materials used to be sharply differentiated from digital services, "but now we're trying to look holistically, and at least in the area of cataloging and metadata, those are moving a lot closer together." Today, in many functional areas the library "doesn't necessarily have a dedicated technical specialist, but we're starting to set expectations that everybody should be able to do the first or second level of work in that space, with patrons, or with computers, or with digital objects." In the reference and instruction area, for example, "our role is now more about the specialized information requests or teaching people with various levels of skill with technology" to perform a wide range of tasks, from constructing advanced search queries to applying for jobs online.

For Leonard, the overarching question today is "Are we delivering the same level of service" for material and digital objects? In managing digital objects specifically, the question becomes "Is the object ready, is it accessible, is it described well, and is it used well," regardless of type or format? In working toward this goal, Leonard emphasizes the value of collaboration between units within the library, and yet it's BPL's "external partnerships that have really made our successes come alive," enabling the library to achieve goals with technology and digital assets that "we would not have been able to do at scale without partners at the table," especially IA, DC, and DPLA. Looking ahead, Leonard points to changes in technology as a key driver of innovation for the library: "As we upgrade systems or choose new platforms, there are opportunities to think about what comes next."

REPOSITORY

A prime example of how technological change has shaped BPL's digital strategy is the development of the repository system underpinning DC. After the BPL-DC partnership was established, BPL hired two software developers to replace DC's earlier DSpace system with a new repository based on Fedora. This decision coincided with BPL's joining the Hydra Project, a collaborative effort to implement Fedora with a stable repository application designed specifically for LAMs. Crucially, Hydra is designed to enable multiple displays or access points for collections, as separate Hydra "heads," that draw resources from a common storage repository. This open source framework is designed to be highly flexible and scalable, such that it can support both the DC repository and BPL's own digital collections, including maps digitized by the Leventhal Map collection, which is global in scope as opposed to the Massachusetts focus of DC.

Beyond the role of technology in driving innovation, BPL has found that changes to the physical space of the library can also have a direct impact on how the institution thinks about the digital as well as the material experiences people may have as they use the library. In 2016, BPL completed a major renovation of its main Central Library facility in Boston, which enabled it to upgrade its digital services for patrons and facilities for digital projects. Leonard says, "As we renovate spaces, there's an opportunity to think about what level of investment is necessary to make something come alive through technology for the in-person experience."

CONCLUSION

As BPL looks to the future, an important question is how to structure the organization to further innovation and adapt to a changing environment. Leonard asks whether it's best to have a "dedicated team focused on some aspect of the larger challenge," or, alternatively, innovation must be infused through "the overall culture" to be effective in moving the institution forward, in which case, "how do you facilitate and support that within existing staff constraints?" Leonard believes that the latter approach "may be more sustainable over time, but there are points where a dedicated team is what you need. So I ultimately support a blend of both models." In fact, this has been the pattern at BPL over the past decade or so as the library has scaled up its digitization services in support of DC, while at the same time working to foster a culture of collaboration and an openness to new ideas throughout the library. Leonard notes that BPL librarians are keen to try out new ideas such as the Bibliocycle, a pedal-powered bookmobile that began in 2014 as an outreach tool for local community events. "The thing that holds us back most is resource availability" rather than ideas and librarians' willingness to experiment. The problem is simply that "technology is not cheap, especially considering that society has come to expect the comfort and responsiveness of Facebook, Amazon, Twitter, etc. That's very difficult for an individual library to compete with." However, Leonard is confident that large-scale collaboration could help bridge the gap between Silicon Valley and the LAM sector. "If you took all of the workers who have a technology job description in all of the public libraries, then you have about the same-size cohort as Facebook." From an institutional point of view, "the power is there, but it would require collaboration at a new level to really make it come alive." For a library that began with a bold, if not "crazy," ambition in the mid-1800s, BPL continues to show how innovative thinking can keep LAMs at the forefront of both digital and material culture in the twenty-first century.

NOTES

1. Boston Public Library, accessed August 5, 2018, http://www.bpl.org.
2. Thanks to Christine Abram, Mary Gumpert, and Mary Pettengill, who interviewed Tom Blake and Danny Pucci.
3. Helena Zinkham and Michelle Springer, "Taking Photographs to the People: The Flickr Commons Project and the Library of Congress," in *A Different Kind of Web: New Connections between Archives and Our Users*, ed. Kate Theimer (Chicago: Society of American Archivists, 2011), 102–15.
4. Martin R. Kalfatovic et al., "Smithsonian Team Flickr: A Library, Archives, and Museums Collaboration in Web 2.0 Space," *Archival Science* 8, no. 4 (December 2008): 268.

Part III

Strategic Use of Resources

Chapter Nine

The Victoria and Albert Museum

Collaboration for Better Collections Access

Martha R. Mahard

The Victoria and Albert Museum (V&A) in London, a sprawling national museum dedicated to art and design, dates back to the early Victorian era. Described by former director Sir Roy Strong as "an extremely capacious handbag,"[1] unlike a more typical art museum, it collects utilitarian objects, items of material culture and fashion, and painting and sculpture from many cultures. It has recently added the collection of born-digital objects, software, and "apps" to its mandate, presenting a whole new array of challenges for description, preservation, and display. In 2008 sixteen members of the V&A staff participated in one of a series of workshops sponsored by OCLC. The workshops were intended to study the possibilities for collaboration across libraries, archives, and museums within a common administrative structure. The OCLC study was published in 2009 as *Beyond the Silos of the LAMs: Collaboration among Libraries, Archives and Museums.*[2] Based on the collaborations suggested in this report, I wanted to follow up and see how the goals articulated in 2008 had been realized.

INTERVIEWS

To gather insights into how the museum's approach to collaboration in the area of collections management had evolved, we interviewed Marion Crick, head of collection management since 2014. Her work involved ensuring institutional conformance with national accreditation standards, developing a management plan for digital acquisitions, and working with curatorial departments implementing the new collection management software. We spoke to other curatorial staff members to gain further insights into how the changes were implemented and their impact on daily operations.

HISTORY OF V&A

The founding mission of the museum that became today's Victoria and Albert Museum was the education of designers, manufacturers, and the public in the areas of art and design, specifically good design exemplified by outstanding objects of furniture, ceramics, textiles, glass, and metalwork. The museum's first director, Henry Cole, hoped to create public demand for "improvements in the character of our national manufactures."[3] A group of objects chosen from the Great Exhibition of 1851 was purchased by the nation and formed the core of a new Museum of Manufactures, which opened its doors in 1852. This first incarnation of the V&A enjoyed the support of Prince Albert and was soon given responsibility for the Government School of Design (founded in 1837). As the fledgling museum quickly outgrew its original quarters in Marlborough House, it became a part of Prince Albert's vision of a grand cultural district to be developed in the area of London rechristened as South Kensington.

The early story of the V&A is one of continued growth and expansion from the time of its opening onward. The collections continued to grow at a pace that regularly exceeded the space available. A mere five years after opening, the collection moved into a series of buildings at the new site, and in June 1857 it became the South Kensington Museum. The next forty years saw the addition of galleries, the North and South courts, a lecture hall, new arts and science schools, residences for senior staff, and, perhaps most important of all, refreshment rooms. The expanding building required changes in infrastructure as well, and elaborate, innovative new systems for controlling lighting, heating, and ventilation were introduced. In the early 1890s, architect Aston Webb was selected "to bring coherence to a site full of awkward gaps and decaying houses left over from the Brompton Park era."[4] Finally, in 1899 Queen Victoria laid the foundation stone for the new complex, and the museum's name was changed to honor the queen and her late consort. This phase of the museum's building was completed in 1909.

Throughout the twentieth century, the museum struggled to expand without adding to its external footprint, reconfiguring internal spaces, making two stories out of old high-ceilinged spaces, and often obliterating the elaborate decorations of the Victorian era. By the end of the twentieth century, the existing fabric was in need of extensive repair and improvement. A major, £150 million renovation program was announced in 2001.[5] In 2017, the V&A's new Exhibition Road Quarters opened, providing a new entrance, courtyard, and dedicated gallery for temporary exhibitions. The recent work includes the restoration of some of the original Victorian design elements, including previously hidden facades by Aston Webb.

FUTUREPLAN

The ambitious program of transformation begun in 2001 as FuturePlan continues to bring new galleries, reimagined spaces, study areas, and visitor amenities to the South Kensington site. "FuturePlan is an ambitious programme of development which is transforming the V&A. The best contemporary designers are creating exciting new galleries and visitor facilities, while revealing and restoring the beauty of the original building. In the past 15 years, over 85% of the Museum's public spaces have been transformed, improving access and allowing the collections to be more elegantly and intelligently displayed. By introducing bold new architectural interventions, FuturePlan aims to delight and to inspire visitors, and to continue the Museum's tradition of championing new talent."[6]

The 2017 completion of the V&A's Exhibition Road Quarters marked "a major milestone in the second phase of FuturePlan."[7] This highly visible and dramatic accomplishment caps years of work affecting the entire physical complex and the management of the museum collections as well. According to the museum's website, the first phase, from 2001 to 2009, completed forty-three projects that "transformed 26,500 square metres and reclaimed 3,000 square metres of back of house space for galleries and public areas. To realise this, the V&A worked with over 50 architectural, design and engineering practices."[8] The collections today make up the world's largest museum of decorative arts and design, with a permanent collection that exceeds 4.5 million objects.

The European galleries, the V&A shop, the Members' Room, and the Weston Cast Court are among the most visible areas revitalized as part of FuturePlan's long-range scheme. In support of the extensive physical upgrades and improvements, the museum's website has also seen a major redesign as part of the focus on outreach and design excellence.

STRATEGIC PLANS AND ORGANIZATION

Sir Mark Jones, V&A director from 2001 to 2011, oversaw significant reorganization and strategic planning. Before Jones's tenure began, the museum had experienced a "sharp fall in visitor numbers," noted a National Audit Office (NAO) report published in February 2001,[9] and reversing this trend became a priority. Although it was not entirely clear that this reduction in visitors was unique to the V&A at the time, other peer institutions did not appear to suffer as significant a drop. Difficulties in standardization of reporting methods and inconsistencies in performance measures were cited as problems with the statistics. But the museum administration recognized a need to improve its "brand awareness" and to make extensive improvements to the fabric of the institution. In its efforts to reach different types of visitors, the museum experimented with longer opening hours and conducted a number of visitor surveys.

One significant move toward improving visitor numbers was made in December 2001 when the admission charges were abolished. In January 2002, the *Guardian* reported that the number of visits had doubled since the ending of the entrance fees.[10] Interestingly, the current director of the V&A, Tristram Hunt, while still a Labour member of Parliament, in 2011 advocated for a reinstitution of admission charges at museums. After his appointment to succeed Martin Roth in 2016, the museum quickly issued assurances that the new director was committed to the principle of free entry.[11]

Another strategy developed in response to the 2001 NAO report included a commitment to "improve the impact of the web site, broaden access to collections, . . . [and] improve public understanding of the nature of the V&A collections."[12] Underlining the speed with which technology drives change, the redesigned website launched in April 2016 was billed as a complete rebuild, not a refresh, of a five-year-old earlier version. The aims remain the same as those articulated in the NAO report: namely, to inspire more people to visit the museum and to define the V&A brand online.[13]

Among the major rearrangements of staff and departments initiated under Mark Jones was the creation of the Word and Image Department. The website describes this amalgamation as responsible for "the Museum's collections of prints, drawings, paintings, photographs, designs, digital art, books and archives, including 8 of the V&A's 18 national collections."[14] Those eight national collections include Architectural Drawings, Art of Photography, British Watercolours and Drawings, Commercial Graphics (including Posters), Digital Art, the National Art Library, Pastels, and Portrait Miniatures.

The Word and Image Department was not the only department created by the amalgamation of widely diverse smaller departments. The museum is now organized around very broad curatorial or administrative functions. The curatorial divisions are combined into three major clusters: the Asian Department; the Furniture, Textiles & Fashion Department; and Sculpture, Metalwork, Ceramics & Glass. These complexes of collecting departments are further divided into display areas. In direct support of the curatorial departments are the Conservation, Exhibitions, Learning, Research, Photographic Studio, and Information Systems Services departments. Administration lies with the Directorate, Development, Estate, Security & Visitor Services, and Technical Services departments. In such an intricate setting, the creation of a single collection management system might seem an unrealizable ideal.

WEBSITE AND DIGITIZATION

In the 2008 OCLC-sponsored workshops, sixteen members of the V&A staff "reaffirmed the importance of gathering, creating and sharing resources among V&A staff, researchers and audiences as vital to the institution's mission. To accomplish these activities more effectively, a strategic approach to digitizing collections was deemed necessary so that information can be accessed more broadly and readily for research, enrichment and innovation. Staff perceive the Web site as a critical destination for these activities and want to position the V&A on the Web as the leading virtual museum of art and design."[15]

The vision of the website as a strategic component in making the collections accessible for research marks a shift from the early 2000s when websites were typically the purview of marketing divisions. During the OCLC workshop, the V&A staff identified two collaborative projects that they viewed as critical to moving the museum closer to its goals. One was described as a "large-scale digitization effort (referred to as the 'Ground Floor Plan')." The idea was to digitize everything on the ground floor of the building, crossing many different departments and featuring items most frequently seen by visitors to the museum, thereby achieving a "critical mass" of digital images "needed to develop broader and richer digital resources across collecting areas."[16] The second recommendation urged the development of "innovative uses of content in a web environment to encourage creativity in art and design and build community among users."[17]

Achieving a critical mass of digital content for websites was a preoccupation of many large cultural heritage institutions in the first decade of the new century. Curators and administrators wrestled with the conflicting benefits of selecting highlights of their collections versus digitizing everything. Although perhaps difficult to imagine today, the prohibitive costs of storage, lack of high-quality viewing equipment, and constantly moving target of imaging technology kept many collecting institutions from making the leap into uncertain territory. Indeed, many institutions that embraced early imaging technologies such as laser disks and Kodak's proprietary PhotoCD found themselves saddled with unusable media within five years. Most of that digital photography had to be done again.

In 2002, what was then the V&A's Theatre Museum (now the Theatre & Performance collection) received a substantial grant to support digitization and website creation featuring a small number of important objects, to be called PeoplePlayUK. To tell the stories of the diverse range of objects in their collection, the curators planned to use supporting items and documentation from other departments within the museum, including the library and the archives. The terms of the grant required that object descriptions comply with the Dublin Core standard, which uses a minimal set of data far more compact than typical museum descriptive records. The Theatre Museum staff found they would not have the time (within the limits of the grant) to create records "of the standards required by the V&A's in-house cataloging systems."[18] Part of the difficulty was that the materials would have to be described in three different V&A systems. To work around this difficulty, they created a dedicated database to contain their small set of object records (fifteen hundred items) as well as the supporting documentation and image metadata. Although the site proved popular, it was ultimately unsustainable, and the content was eventually absorbed into the V&A website, without the original site's features. The problem of the multiple databases and separately maintained cataloging systems—of which the Theatre Museum's was but one example—eventually became too problematic to ignore, and developing a museum-wide collection management system became a strategic imperative.

DIGITAL FUTUREPLAN

By the time the 2010–2015 strategic plan was written, the upgrading of the museum's collections management system was at a critical point. The entire digital infrastructure needed work, and as the project to redesign the website got underway, the problems involved with bringing together the many incompatible systems and datasets required resolution.

When interviewed in 2015, Marian Crick described her position as having oversight of collections information and systems, or "digital asset management." The museum was committed to the task of assembling and harnessing the various "pockets of digitization" that had developed since early 2002. Like many similar long-established institutions at the time, the V&A was still distinctly siloed, and resistance to change, while not always overt, was a strong factor. Crick's charge also included responsibility for the photographic studio, the existing body of digital images created to document the collection, and the growing body of born-digital acquisitions. By the time of the interview, she and her team had recently completed the development and implementation of the new collections management system. Work on the system had been launched in 2010 as one of the Digital FuturePlan initiatives articulated in the 2010–2015 strategic plan.[19] In 2013, she had been brought in to make sure that the project was successfully concluded by its due date in 2014. The new system needed to be able to manage the V&A's diverse collections in a comprehensive fashion. It was expected to achieve a number of museum-wide efficiencies, including the following:

- Reduction of duplication and reuse of data
- Promotion of simpler and more consistent processes and data management

- Elimination of backlogs in the system
- Introduction of savings on licenses and IT management systems[20]

Although much had been done to eliminate department silos by bringing many smaller curatorial areas into four major collecting departments, the departments had their own procedures and cataloging practices, as well as homegrown databases, as we have seen. Crick noted that part of her work had been to eliminate as many of these as possible by bringing them into the new collection management system and ensuring that the new system could interact with the legacy systems that continued in use. She noted, "We can't expect the collections management system to do absolutely everything that everyone needs. We don't want to build the full function of a few offices into the collections management system. But the collections management system needs to be able to talk to all the other applications."

Crick described the process through which the staff of the museum's diverse collecting departments were involved in the changes to the collection management system and the new roles that her department had assumed. She had to be a persuasive advocate for changes to which the museum administration was committed and work across curatorial departments to demonstrate the value of a more complex digital asset management system. To this end, she and her team conducted open meetings for the museum staff on a regular basis. Attended by more than 150 staff members, these meetings helped to foster a sense of ownership and buy-in to the proposed new system. One department worked through an elaborate review and documentation of its existing workflow. In the course of this exercise, its staff discovered for themselves areas where their processes were antiquated, duplicative, or inefficient. This knowledge contributed to the development of the asset management system, and participants were able to see firsthand how the new system could improve their work process.

In addition to containing traditional descriptive information about the objects in the collections, the new system also functioned as a project management tool, enabling conservators, exhibition planners, designers, and others to access collections data for resource planning. The new collection management system can combine data about the acquisition of an object with its exhibition information and conservation history. Crick explained,

> The work around resource planning is using the information that we have within our collections management system about those planned exhibitions, about the objects that are planned for use in those exhibitions, you know, how much conservation they need, how many people they need to move it, what will they need to mount, when will they need to be photographed for the exhibition, and it's all being captured through our collections management workflow, which is what we at the collections management program developed. . . . [It's all] about managing those physical objects through a specific set

> of processes that you have to do both organizationally and legally to get your work done.

Among her many responsibilities Crick is also charged with getting the museum through the accreditation process, required in the United Kingdom every three years. It was therefore essential to her that the collection management system address the nine primary procedures required for accreditation as outlined in the Collections Trust's Spectrum (5.0) standard:

- Object entry
- Acquisition and accessioning
- Location and movement control
- Inventory
- Cataloging
- Object exit
- Loans in (borrowing objects)
- Loans out (lending objects)
- Documentation planning

The latest version of Spectrum (5.0) was published in September 2017 and is available on the Collections Trust website.[21] Although a UK standard, it is widely used throughout the European community. The V&A's collection management system follows the Spectrum template closely and is intended to facilitate transparency and accountability in the accreditation process.

The work done by Crick and her associates on the V&A's digital media team in conjunction with the product innovation consultancy MadeByMany resulted in a highly successful and user-friendly front end for the museum's web page, which won the International Design Communication Award for 2016.[22] This successful top layer of user access is visually dramatic and enables simple collection browsing. When one moves into a deeper level of research, however, there is still work to be done. The "Search the Collections" page, accessible from a link in small type at the bottom of the home page, is regularly updated, but the look and feel still reflect the website's earlier incarnation. It looks tacked on to the more dazzling upper layer. The 2016–2017 annual report provided the welcome news that the "Search the Collections" feature "will be the next area to the V&A's digital presence to be reinterpreted to bring it into line with a twenty-first-century vision of the V&A."[23]

CONCLUSION

The V&A OCLC workshop participants recognized the need for a widely representative body of digital content to make the museum's holdings available online. They also recognized that the website would be a major entry point for far more users than would ever actually cross the threshold on Exhibition Road. The museum's "brand" demanded a well-designed, possibly cutting-edge, online entry point that would immediately support its eminence in the field of material culture and design. In the years that followed the OCLC workshop, enormous progress was made in providing online access to the V&A's collections. A recent "Search the Collections" page of the website claimed 1,192,282 objects and 723,566 images available for searching online.[24] The system is in place; now the curatorial departments must begin to standardize their cataloging practices and bring their enormous legacy of collections data forward to meet current user expectations for access and retrieval. This is likely to be a much longer and more arduous process.

NOTES

1. Roy Strong, widely quoted, most authoritatively in the *Oxford Dictionary of Art & Artists*, ed. Ian Chilvers (Oxford: Oxford University Press, 2015).
2. Diane M. Zorich, Günter Waibel, and Ricky Erway, *Beyond the Silos of the LAMs* (Dublin, OH: OCLC, 2008).
3. "Building the Museum," V&A, accessed January 20, 2018, https://www.vam.ac.uk/articles/building-the-museum.
4. "Building the Museum."
5. "V&A to Have £150m Facelift," *BBC News*, April 18, 2002, accessed January 20, 2018, http://news.bbc.co.uk/2/hi/entertainment/1937015.stm.
6. "FuturePlan," V&A, accessed April 2, 2018, https://www.vam.ac.uk/info/futureplan.
7. "Completed FuturePlan Projects," V&A, accessed April 2, 2018, https://www.vam.ac.uk/info/futureplan-completed-projects.
8. "Completed FuturePlan Projects."
9. John Bourn, "Access to the Victoria and Albert Museum," National Audit Office, February 22, 2001, accessed January 20, 2018, https://www.nao.org.uk/report/access-to-the-victoria-and-albert-museum.
10. Fiachra Gibbons, "Visits Double with End of Museum Charges," *Guardian*, January 7, 2002, accessed April 2, 2018, https://www.theguardian.com/uk/2002/jan/07/arts.highereducation.
11. Mark Brown, "V&A Reiterates Commitment to Free Entry after Tristram Hunt Appointment," *Guardian*, January 13, 2017, accessed July 26, 2018, https://www.theguardian.com/artanddesign/2017/jan/13/va-reiterates-commitment-to-free-entry-after-tristram-hunt-appointment.
12. John Bourn, "Access to the Victoria and Albert Museum," Report by the Comptroller and Auditor General, National Audit Office, February 22, 2001, accessed January 20, 2018, https://www.nao.org.uk/wp-content/uploads/2001/02/0001238.pdf, p. 5.
13. Kati Price, "The New V&A Website," *V&A Blog*, April 12, 2016, accessed April 2, 2018, http://www.vam.ac.uk/blog/digital-media/new-website.
14. "Word and Image Department," V&A, accessed October 13, 2017, http://www.vam.ac.uk/content/articles/w/word-and-image-department.
15. Zorich, Waibel, and Erway, *Beyond the Silos of the LAMs*, 49.
16. Zorich, Waibel, and Erway, *Beyond the Silos of the LAMs*, 50.
17. Zorich, Waibel, and Erway, *Beyond the Silos of the LAMs*.
18. Claire Hudson, "The Digital Museum," in *Evaluating and Measuring the Value, Use and Impact of Digital Collections*, ed. Lorna M. Hughes (London: Facet Publishing, 2012), 37.

19. "Strategic Plan, 2010–2015: 2010/11," V&A, accessed April 2, 2018, http://media.vam.ac.uk/media/documents/about-us/2010/v&a-strategicplan2010-15.pdf.
20. Item 8 of "Board of Trustees, Minutes," V&A, November 20, 2014, accessed January 20, 2018, http://www.vam.ac.uk/__data/assets/pdf_file/0018/252513/November-2015-minutes.pdf.
21. "Spectrum," Collections Trust, accessed March 13, 2018, https://collectionstrust.org.uk/spectrum.
22. Department for Digital, Culture, Media & Sport and Victoria and Albert Museum, "Victoria and Albert Museum Annual Report and Accounts 2016 to 2017," GOV.UK, July 19, 2017, accessed March 13, 2018, https://www.gov.uk/government/publications/victoria-and-albert-museum-annual-report-and-accounts-2016-to-2017.
23. Department for Digital, Culture, Media & Sport and Victoria and Albert Museum, "Victoria and Albert Museum Annual Report and Accounts 2016 to 2017."
24. "Search the Collections," V&A, accessed April 13, 2018, https://collections.vam.ac.uk.

Chapter Ten

The National Library of Australia

Digital Assets as a Driver for Change in a National Library

Ross Harvey and Jaye Weatherburn

The National Library of Australia (NLA) provides a leading example of innovation and leadership, in Australia and internationally, and is highly effective at managing and making available its digital assets. The NLA has a long history of digital innovation: examples include the Australian National Bibliographic Database (http://www.nla.gov.au/librariesaustralia/about/anbd), established in 1981 under this name and based on an earlier MARC record database established in 1974; PANDORA (http://pandora.nla.gov.au), one of the first web archives in the world, established in 1996; and Trove (trove.nla.gov.au), a collaborative platform that provides access to resources in both the NLA and many other Australian cultural and research institutions.

This case study focuses on an institution that has exhibited leadership in applying digital technology and in collaborating across disciplinary and institutional boundaries. This study of the NLA has the primary goal of elucidating the ways in which proliferating digital content is changing how cultural heritage organizations organize and use information. It does this by examining how the NLA is creating, collecting, organizing, exhibiting, and preserving digital information to identify the keys to its success. In particular, it

- describes a strong culture of extensive, integrated collaboration,
- highlights the importance of maintaining a strong IT capability and building in-house systems to meet its needs,
- identifies the value of developing skills by focused recruitment and growing staff capabilities,

- notes why embracing an "end-to-end process" concept is essential,
- emphasizes the need to foster a culture of innovation, and
- notes the growing role of the user in providing better access to digital resources.

Collaboration among libraries, archives, and museums (LAMs) has become an increasingly important activity as large and small repositories have struggled to meet the demand for online access to collections and to respond to new institutional demands for data management and digital preservation services. Many smaller institutions are still taking their initial, experimental steps in digital curation, and even large institutions find it difficult to sustain their digital services. The NLA is somewhat unusual in that it combines library, archives, and museum functions to successfully manage its digital assets. Collaboration is a key factor in the NLA's successful contribution to Australian culture, demonstrated in its service charter: "By offering a strong national focus in all that we do and cooperating with others who share our goals, we support learning and creative and intellectual endeavour and contribute to the vitality of Australian culture and heritage."[1]

BACKGROUND

The NLA was formally established in 1960 through the National Library Act of that year but has a much longer history dating back to the Commonwealth Parliamentary Library established in 1901. Its website describes its aim as "to ensure that documentary resources of national significance relating to Australia and the Australian people, as well as significant non-Australian library materials, are collected, preserved and made accessible either through the library or through collaborative arrangements with other libraries and information providers."[2]

To meet the demands of its role, the NLA employs four hundred staff and manages a collection of about ten million items, including books, journals, newspapers, music scores, maps, e-resources, websites, manuscripts (personal papers and organizational archives), documentary pictures, and oral history and folklore recordings. As of June 2016 it had digitized over 251,000 items (many of them containing multiple pieces) and over 21.75 million pages of newspapers. Its websites received almost twenty-eight million visits in 2015 and 2016. The library's digitized collections totaled more than 4.8 petabytes in June 2016.[3]

The NLA collects material in a wide range of formats. Its collections include a large manuscript collection, and its pictures collection includes photographs, prints, drawings, watercolors, cartoons, miniatures, paintings, architectural plans, objects, and sculptures. In order to manage this wide range of formats, the NLA inevitably has had to adopt practices from archives and museums. The organizational structure consists of six divisions:

- Collections Management
- Australian Collections and Reader Services
- National Collections Access
- Executive and Public Programs
- Information Technology
- Corporate Services

The first three divisions relate to "core library business," with the assistant director-general of information technology, David Wong, describing the importance of centralizing the information technology division "so that we can scale up and down as required to meet the needs of the organization."

The NLA has for many years performed a leadership role nationally in developing and managing collaborative online services with the Australian library community. The aim is to enhance access to online resources for users throughout Australia, indeed the world, and to do this the NLA developed Trove, a system that harvests and aggregates metadata and content from across the LAM sector into one online platform. Trove is a centralized national service built with the collaboration of major Australian libraries. The service is able to locate resources about Australia and Australians and reaches many locations otherwise unavailable to external search engines.

INTERVIEWS

We conducted semistructured interviews in person with six key staff of the NLA in December 2015. Each interview lasted about forty-five minutes. To cover a range of views, we interviewed personnel selected from different units. The interviewees were

Amelia Mackenzie, assistant director-general of collections management
David Wong, assistant director-general of information technology
Wan Wong, director of digitization and photography
Cornel Platzer, director of preservation services
Deirdre Kiorgaard, director of Trove
Kevin Bradley, senior curator of research collections and unpublished materials

Each interview was recorded and transcribed, and the transcriptions were provided to the interviewees for verification. Questions for the interviews were tailored specifically for each of the different units identified above. The questions are provided in appendix A.

Questions for high-level administration focused on mission, vision, and strategy for the library, particularly for creating and managing digital assets. We aimed to discover how the library intends to evolve and manage digital challenges and changes in technology over the next five to ten years and whether a centralized or decentralized approach is preferred. We investigated collaboration within and outside the library, institutional challenges and innovation, and priorities for digitization and online access, and we examined resource constraints and funding sources to support digital initiatives.

Questions for IT staff focused on systems, workflows, and processes, both existing and being implemented, particularly for management of digital assets and access. We asked about if and how any digital preservation plans are being implemented and investigated how collaboration works in terms of managing IT infrastructure and services. We sought information about vendor services versus in-house development and also inquired about future challenges and innovations that could impact the library as a whole.

Questions for curators, collection managers, and metadata specialists included seeking details about current digital assets managed, digitization efforts, workflows and procedures for managing digital assets, and metadata schemas and standards used. We sought information about the key technologies and plans for preservation and asked about the evolution of the library's assets over the next five to ten years. We also focused on collaboration within the library and asked about challenges faced, including resource constraints and organizational factors.

THEMES

Six themes were identified and are explained in the rest of this case study:

1. Creating a strong culture of extensive, integrated collaboration
2. Developing skills through focused recruitment and by growing staff capabilities
3. Maintaining a strong IT capability and building in-house systems
4. Embracing an "end-to-end process" concept
5. Fostering innovation
6. Keeping pace with the growing role of the user

Creating a Strong Culture of Extensive, Integrated Collaboration

One theme identified by all interviewees and strongly apparent from the first interview was the extent of collaboration present in the NLA, both internally and with other organizations, and its importance for what the NLA is achieving in effectively managing its digital assets. Although there was a long history of significant collaboration across all sections of the library, the need to embrace things digital was the catalyst for increased activity. The "end-to-end process" approach requires extensive, integrated collaboration and a high level of teamwork with full engagement from all participants. This teamwork was consciously developed in 1998 when the NLA decided it needed to engage fully with digital resources. The senior curator of research collections and unpublished materials, Kevin Bradley, noted that the then director-general, Warren Horton, announced that the NLA would be going digital, and in its early stages the process was one of getting people together to discuss the challenges involved in managing digital materials. Meetings were convened that aimed to reach understandings about what was required to become increasingly digital and to identify the many dependencies that needed to be put in place.

The consequence was that collaboration developed because of the need to make strong cases to others in the same division and also in other divisions. Several interviewees made the point that this was not just an initial activity limited to the start of a new process: it is ongoing.

Collaboration is the key to effective management of digital information within the NLA. No one division of the NLA can do it all. One division can acquire, process, and organize digital materials, but other divisions are involved in their preservation, management, and documentation. This requires negotiation to achieve the "end-to-end process" and "whole life cycle," terms frequently used by interviewees.

The assistant director-general of collections management, Amelia Mackenzie, provided the example of digital preservation to illustrate the interconnectedness of processes within the library. "As we've begun to implement the systems and workflows that we need for that, it's become really clear to everybody how digital preservation just is the spine that runs through all of our collection management activities." In addition to mentioning a greater awareness of "the connectedness of preservation at all points of a collection and a collecting life cycle," Mackenzie indicated that collaboration has increased to enable "a shared understanding of the whole life cycle amongst all the staff at every point of the chain." It has become a "necessity of all of the participants in the life cycle to understand the whole life cycle." An outcome of the increased shared understanding is that "the boundaries between our divisions have become quite blurred."

Collaboration within the library is facilitated by formal mechanisms, as well as informal actions. The director of digitization and photography, Wan Wong, noted "formal communication mechanisms," such as a digitization committee with representation from other divisions of the library: collection areas, preservation, public outreach, and Trove. Wan Wong also noted that meetings between the digitization branch and each collection area, with preservation staff also attending, act as "an ongoing monitoring of what materials are being digitized, what are the problems." Informal collaboration methods are also powerful: "We just can walk down the stairs and talk to people if you need to," added David Wong.

The NLA has a long history of effective collaboration with other libraries, perhaps best exemplified by the history of collaboration devolving from the Australian Bibliographic Network, which "sort of became part of Australian libraries' DNA," according to Mackenzie. Interviewees also frequently noted the example of Trove. For example, Wan Wong stated, "The library's efforts are heavily invested in Trove. . . . Over the next five to ten years I expect Trove will continue to grow and be a shared delivery system in the sense that other libraries will contribute to maintaining Trove so they can use Trove for delivery of their digital collections and not have to create and maintain their own."

Interviewees noted three areas where collaboration between Trove and organizations outside the NLA occurred. Wan Wong indicated that one is collaboration with contributors of material digitized by the NLA, which manages a newspaper digitization program "based on strong collaborations with state and territory libraries who supply the microfilm as original material for capture." Another is collaboration with the content partners of Trove: "the organizations, galleries, archives, museums, historical societies, institutional repositories and organizations like the ABC [Australian Broadcasting Corporation] that we've been working with." Collaboration with institutions other than libraries is relatively new for the NLA. The third area is with what Trove director Deirdre Kiorgaard calls "our siblings, which are Europeana, Digital NZ, and DPLA [Digital Public Library of America]."

Developing Skills through Focused Recruitment and by Growing Staff Capabilities

One reason for the effectiveness of the NLA's management of digital assets is the skills it can call on among NLA staff. This has been consciously developed through focused recruitment and strategies to grow staff capabilities.

Staff employed by the NLA demonstrate a wide range of skills. "They've all got different backgrounds, different work histories before coming here," observed Kiorgaard. In addition to specialist skills they should ideally also possess what one interviewee called "good system aptitude . . . [comfort] with systems which do crazy things and systems that might break down and keep changing." "Generic skills" that all staff should have included attention to detail, flexibility, an ability to see relationships between different systems, and an understanding of how data comes from one place to another and displays to the user, according to Wan Wong.

Digital skills were considered especially important. The director of preservation services, Cornel Platzer, indicated that all the positions advertised by the NLA include "a criterion about digital skills and being capable in that area," and all staff need to know about "how to leverage technology and systems in order to support the work that they're doing."

Staff at the NLA tend to stay a long time there, so attention has been paid to refocusing and building skills. Mackenzie commented that staff with "traditional library skills" need to be moved "up into a digital environment" and described a digital skills program, where staff are seconded to create and deliver training. This started several years ago with basic training in areas such as the types of e-book formats. At the start these sessions introduced staff to "new" technologies such as iPads. "They called them petting zoos, where you could come and try out any of these devices," said Mackenzie, adding that the aim has been to change the mind-set so that, as more staff deal with digital content, they can appreciate and understand "what digital actually means for us in the library and what the issues are."

This theme of building skills for working with digital materials was reiterated in relation to specialist skills. One approach was to identify the knowledge that was hard to get and appoint personnel with that knowledge, then train them in what else they needed to know. The example was given of a position that required both specific IT-focused skill sets and knowledge of archival principles. The deep understanding of archival principles is less common than the specific IT-focused skill sets, so the person appointed should have the archival knowledge and could, if necessary, be trained in IT skills.

Maintaining a Strong IT Capability and Building In-House Systems

The NLA places high value on its IT staff. IT is centralized and well supported, which allows the library, noted David Wong, "to continue the strategic focus of our IT development over the next five to ten years, shaped to the organization's mission. Because it's quite critical to us." The IT budget is about 10 percent of the NLA's total budget, which as a proportion is quite high for a small to medium-size organization. David Wong indicated that despite this level of resourcing the NLA is "challenged resource wise and skills wise because, as you know, digital is big. Going from digitizing physical to born-digital material, the volume's increasing, the formats are. There's a wide range of materials and content types." Other challenges come from changing user demands; David Wong noted, "People expect more over time. People don't just expect us to collect, but to provide access to things. People wanting enriched data. People want things like Twitter feeds and Facebook content to be collected and that's tough because you know data's alive and it's moving around."

The centralization of IT services has advantages for the library. David Wong suggested it allows flexibility: "We can scale up and down as required to meet the needs of the organization." When the head of the IT division retired in 2015, a conscious strategic decision was made by the director-general to advertise the position as "a head of IT" to continue the strategic focus of IT development in the library over the next five to ten years, according to Mackenzie.

The NLA operates a complex range of systems: traditional library systems such as the library catalog with its internal systems and its public interface; the national bibliographic database, a union catalog for Australian libraries; and the "digital library space, mainly a set of bespoke systems that we've developed internally" for digitization, workflow management, and delivery, noted David Wong. This includes Trove, a system built internally to provide access, free-text search, and enriched data with text corrections and the like. Within the digital library space, third-party systems are integrated, such as Archivists' Toolkit.

The NLA's systems are constantly evolving. At the time when the interviews were conducted, the Digital Library Infrastructure Replacement (DLIR) program to replace aging collection management systems was well underway. Kiorgaard commented, "As an organization, we knew we had these once leading-edge but now outdated backend systems that were going to die, and we were going to lose digital resources if we didn't do something." Kiorgaard considered that the DLIR project has been a major catalyst for developing the "end-to-end process" thinking referred to earlier: "It's not just the ingestion and creation of digital objects. It doesn't stop there. Once you've got them, yes, you might be able to preserve them, but who cares, really, if you can't actually get anybody to them. . . . If you don't collect or create the right metadata, then you're not going to be able to provide good navigation down the end of the line."

Platzer described the DLIR process. In 2012, the library "went out to market looking for an end-to-end solution for managing digital content. It was fairly ambitious in what it was seeking. . . . They didn't identify any other systems [apart from two, Preservica and Doc Supply] that met their needs, and at that point the National Library determined that it needed to develop its own in-house capability in terms of systems and so on, either through replacing systems that were no longer up to contemporary expectations or developing new systems to meet those needs." The DLIR was scheduled to be completed in June 2017.[4]

The National Library is "very good at building" in-house systems, Wan Wong commented, and Platzer added that the "approach within the organization is agile, so that means that it's a process of, 'Is this working? How well is it working?' If it's not working, then we change it." David Wong noted that the NLA started building in-house systems about fifteen years ago with its Digital Collection Manager, which "manages digitization and also the content after it's been digitized," and PANDORA, a system developed for web archiving. The level of development of bespoke systems is "slightly unusual for most major institutions," according to Mackenzie: much of it is innovative; there are no products on the market that do what the bespoke systems do. The high level of in-house development attracts "good IT people because they're very motivated to work on this stuff."

The library is currently heavily focused on the development of Trove, which Platzer describes as "the delivery system for the library's digital assets, [which] also aggregates metadata for material from across the GLAM[5] sector."

Embracing an "End-to-End Process" Concept

An institution the size and complexity of the NLA has collections that are closer to those in galleries and museums and not limited to library materials. In this, the NLA is no different from other national libraries, such as the Library of Congress and the British Library. The development of Trove means that the NLA aggregates content from not just libraries but museums, galleries, archives, historical societies, and institutional repositories as well. The traditional distinctions between kinds of material are reduced as the need to manage them in a digital library increases. Individual differences are, of course, still important. The NLA's digital library operations require a centralized system that is built on standardized workflows.

The section on collaboration, above, noted that interviewees frequently used the terms "end-to-end process" and "whole life cycle." The need to embrace these concepts and implement them in systems has driven major changes at the library, which David Wong has described as a move from a digital asset management system to a digital library system: "The digital library provides the whole of life cycle management, from ingestion, collection management, preservation, and through to access and discovery. Across those functions, digital objects change and grow over time. I guess the difference between a digital library system and a digital asset management system is digital asset management systems manage assets as static immutable objects, whereas in a digital library you update, augment, enrich, and contextualize objects over time." Making the structural changes needed to build a digital library requires that "workflows and systems are optimized and customized to meet business requirements," in David Wong's words. Workflows are simplified as much as possible, but not to the extent that everyone is "forced" into generic workflows. This is where the "end-to-end process" or "whole life cycle" approach comes in.

Although there are changes in systems, with new systems being developed and implemented, the mission of the NLA has not changed. In response to the question "How does digital content relate to your institution's overall mission and vision?" Mackenzie replied, "Our aim has never changed, all of those years. . . . 'Make access happen' is how we express that. . . . It's really—How do we make our collections accessible to Australians, wherever they are. And of course, people beyond Australia." Mackenzie continued that the NLA has "the responsibility and the mandate to collect the Australian cultural record in digital form." Building the collections and providing access to them are the drivers; digital allows this to happen better. Mackenzie said, "Our current strategy for creating and managing digital assets basically is collecting in digital form, digitizing the physical form, creating the appropriate level of metadata for those items, with a view to the long term. We have to be sure that we have enough metadata to last us for many years to come."

Other changes, in addition to systems changes, are required. Platzer suggested that the configuration of the NLA, with its six divisions, may need to change: "The digital imperative has been rolling through, and it's going to be even greater in the coming years. . . . I'm not sure that the model, the structure that the National Library is working under at the moment is the one that will best meet its needs in the future."

The mind-set of staff needs to change as a result of increasing convergence. Although this is happening, Kiorgaard considered it a "difficult battle." "It's hard to say, 'No, you aren't special.'" Kiorgaard gave this example: "Manuscripts are organized hierarchically, in series, folders, and so on. People managing archives and manuscripts think the hierarchical, archival way of dealing with things is unique, and you have to explain, well, actually, journals have articles. Picture albums have individual pages and individual pictures. Ten thousand Hurley negatives didn't come as one blob. Everything has a hierarchical structure, and you have to go 'We're not going to build navigation suited only to your hierarchical structure, it has to be adaptable.' That's been difficult."

Bradley also noted the need for a mind-set change toward a factory-like approach, suggesting that the "end-to-end process" approach demands different ways of thinking about digitization.

Fostering Innovation

The NLA fosters an atmosphere of innovation, Trove being a principal example. David Wong said, "We've had huge success with Trove, Trove Newspapers. That's probably the jewel in the crown." The NLA's digital library is another example: "We kind of see that as a world-leading solution. We've been in the space for fifteen, twenty years, and we don't see any other solution that's as integrated as ours and that provides as rich a collection."

In addition to making digital materials discoverable and visible through Trove, the innovations that the NLA has developed in recent times aim to build end-to-end processes. Due to development of a freely accessible application programming interface (API) and documented examples of how to use it, "twelve hundred people . . . have, at one point, used the API," reported Kiorgaard. Further evidence of the reach of Trove comes from universities encouraging students to use the Trove API and also institutional vendors and researchers using it for different purposes.

Innovations also arise in response to competition. David Wong noted, "We've got competitors in the space . . . Twitter and Facebook." With Twitter and Facebook "the richness is not only with the content but the comments and inferences," and the NLA also needs to provide such services that allow users to participate: "End users expect a lot. They want information to be available instantaneously. They want to be able to engage with the content." David Wong also noted that the NLA has provided users with the tools to correct text, annotate, and tag in Trove, but "we need to do a lot more of that." These services need to be provided "across all our content, and we need to allow people to delve into a manuscript collection and highlight the gem that's hidden right within a collection and no one actually knows about it. We want them to tag that and make that discoverable."

Providing users with these tools also benefits the library. David Wong observed, "There's only so much our curators can do when it comes to describing collections and curating. We're fairly small. We've got a big collection. We've only digitized less than 5 percent of our physical collection. I think we need to make more of it available and allow users to curate the collections, to describe it, to mark it up, and to draw attention to it." In another five to ten years, the library hopes, according to David Wong, to have moved from a position where "the library and curators mediate access to content" to a fully disintermediated model where "the collection is curated by the public and users."

The Trove system's engagement with users has generated a significant amount of content. At the end of 2015 there were more than 50,000 Trove lists, 4 million tags, 100,000 comments, and 180 million lines of newspaper text corrected, reported Kiorgaard, and its rapid growth is demonstrated by the statistics from the end of March 2017: more than 95,000 lists, 4.9 million tags, over 150,000 comments, and 225.6 million lines of newspaper text corrected (updated statistics provided by Wan Wong).

There is inevitably some internal resistance to innovation. The library has been in the "legacy space" for a long time, so the move from legacy workflows and processes to end-to-end processes is "a cultural shift, and there's a lot of resistance to change," observed David Wong.

Keeping Pace with the Growing Role of the User

The growing need to keep up with changing technology in the wider social media space is recognized as an ongoing issue. As David Wong noted, "We've got competitors in the space . . . Twitter and Facebook. If we don't innovate and stay fresh and have user interfaces that are rich and people want to come to, if people don't want to visit our collection, then I think we become irrelevant over time."

To this end, the NLA has embraced the idea of crowdsourcing as an important measure to provide better access in a world of digital deluge. According to David Wong, "Crowdsourcing and using people, the public, to enrich collections is a big thing. There's only so much our curators can do when it comes to describing collections and curating." Harnessing the power of the crowd in this way makes more of the collections available and draws attention to previously hidden resources. Integrating "users" and "customers" more closely into the curation process will help to make library collections more "like some of the services you see on the web now just in general, like Twitter, and Facebook, and YouTube, where the user is a lot more engaged and connected with the content." Users provide "insight and we rely on them to enrich the content" that is contained within collections. "At the moment, the library and curators mediate access to content, but in the future I think it's going to be the public and users mediating access to it and enriching it."

Keeping pace with the evolving role of the user is not only about providing access. It is also important to change the idea of librarians and archivists as "gatekeepers" of information, instead opening up content so that it is available to be linked across the web. This requires a discussion about new roles for curators in the LAM sector, a paradigm shift from manual cataloging to a more automated process using text mining. David Wong provided this comment: "With free-text search, with for example Trove, things are a lot more discoverable and a lot more accessible if you're just using the technology."

CONCLUSION

The NLA's mandate to provide leadership and its culture of innovation are the reasons for its success in managing its digital assets and making them available to Australia and to the world. Its mission has not changed as it has embraced digital content: it continues to collect the Australian cultural record and make its collections accessible to Australians, wherever they are, and to people beyond Australia. Its effectiveness in carrying out this mission is due in large part to factors identified in this case study. A long history of collaboration within the library has allowed it to develop an "end-to-end process" approach for managing digital assets. The NLA recognizes the value of staff development programs and is supported by a centralized IT structure that serves to develop systems to support its mission. It recognizes that an increasing culture of convergence of the traditional collection professions must be embraced in order to best manage collections into the future. The NLA fosters an atmosphere of innovation, the most recent example in a long line of innovations being Trove. Perhaps most importantly, the NLA is actively seeking new ways to meet the challenges involved in managing, preserving, and providing ongoing access to digital materials, including embracing increased user engagement—a mission that seeks to never allow the library to become irrelevant in a constantly changing digital world.

NOTES

1. "Service Charter," National Library of Australia (NLA), accessed July 29, 2018, https://www.nla.gov.au/service-charter.
2. "Service Charter."
3. "Facts and Figures. 2016–17 Snapshot," NLA, accessed July 29, 2018, https://www.nla.gov.au/facts-and-figures.
4. "DLIR Program Details," NLA, accessed July 29, 2018, https://www.nla.gov.au/dlir/project-details.
5. Australian usage is "GLAM" (galleries, libraries, archives, museums) rather than "LAM" (libraries, archives, museums), which is more common in the United States.

Look up Trove for discussion

Part IV

Institutions in Transition

Chapter Eleven

The Leviathan Library and Archives at the Jackman Museum of Modern Art

The Impact of Changing Priorities

Michèle V. Cloonan

This anonymized case study is about a museum that decided to close its library and lay off all the library staff except for the archivist. The decision came as a surprise at the institution because two of the librarians had a stellar record of getting grants for library-museum projects. However, the new director, two donors, and the board of trustees had a vision for the museum, and that vision did not include a library.

INTERVIEWS

What happens when, despite a number of successful and well-funded library initiatives, a museum art library is closed anyway? This is the conundrum that we considered during our initial interview with Georgina Spelvin and Michaela Beaumont, the professional staff of the Leviathan Library and Archives at the Jackman Museum of Modern Art. They described the situation for us. Interviewees, staff, and museum names have been anonymized.

A NEW DIRECTOR AND A NEW DIRECTION

Georgina and Michaela had arranged for a meeting with the new director, Penny Hunt-Moore. She had succeeded the previous head, Art Spencer, an avuncular person, who ran the museum for some twenty years, until he retired the year before. With Art's encouragement, the librarians had applied for (and received) four grants over the past six years: one from the Institute of Museum and Library Services and three from foundations. The grants enabled the museum to provide increased access to the collections through improved cataloging and an integrated online system—which made it possible to search for museum objects, library materials, and manuscripts in one place. This was a major undertaking: the library alone had over fifty thousand books, periodicals, and manuscripts, and the museum had tens of thousands of objects. Additionally, the grants covered Michaela Beaumont's salary and expanded hours for the library. The librarians were excited because one of the foundations had just contacted them about applying for a grant to expand their web-based initiatives.

The librarians were shown into Director Hunt-Moore's office with uncharacteristic formality on the part of the executive assistant, who had worked at the museum for many years. Although the librarians had met the director at several museum events, she seemed to look right past them. Both were struck by the new office interior. Gone were the heavy pieces of mahogany furniture, the plush carpeting, and the portraits of the museum's founders and early directors. In their place was Memphis Milano furniture, a Bridget Riley painting, and a contemporary rug in neutral colors. After extending her hand to each of them rather tentatively, the director announced that they would be joined by the recently hired vice president for employee talent and success, Brian Kent Morris. (The former head of what was previously known as "HR" had left the museum several months after the new director arrived.)

Brian strode in carrying two black folders. They all sat down at the round table in the corner of the office. Hunt-Moore quickly explained that the board had just approved a new strategic plan and that the library was not part of it; it would be closed at the end of the month. The archival assistant, who happened to be the niece of one of the trustees, would be retained to oversee the museum's archives and to answer reference questions from the curators and the public "as needed." Hunt-Moore told the group that she had a meeting downtown and that Brian would go over the particulars. She then left, after promising the librarians that the museum would be happy to write excellent letters of recommendation for them.

Sensing the librarians' shock, Brian thanked them for their service to the museum. Someone from a career outplacement firm would be meeting with them soon, he explained. He handed them the black folders. Their compensation packages were detailed inside. They would receive compensation commensurate with the number of years that each of them had worked at the museum. He explained that it was normal industry practice to escort employees off the premises as soon as they were let go, but in this situation the librarians would be given a month to notify the granting agencies that had supported the library, and the museum would help them to discontinue their grant projects. Brian suggested that they both go home early and meet with the career outplacement advisor the next day.

Georgina had been with the museum for eighteen years and was nearing retirement age. Her first instinct following the stunning news was to get in touch with a lawyer, who confirmed that she could probably sue the museum for age discrimination at the least. Michaela, who was newer to the field, immediately edited her LinkedIn profile. Once they had recovered their equilibrium, they began to direct their energies toward finding jobs elsewhere. Georgina was well known in the field, and both women were active in professional organizations. Michaela had given a number of presentations about her grant-funded projects. They received strong support from their colleagues, some of whom had faced layoffs and cutbacks in their own institutions.

What had happened that led to this decision? Over the next couple of weeks, Georgina and Michaela put all the pieces together based on the museum's history, a recent major gift, and information about the new director.

HISTORY OF THE JACKMAN MUSEUM

The Jackman Museum was founded in the late nineteenth century in a once prosperous city by two leading industrialists and a university president with the vision to collect contemporary art rather than try to build an encyclopedic museum. The museum would be situated near the university, and classes would be held there. (Later the museum was at the forefront of audience engagement.) The museum was always known for its outstanding exhibitions and its active collecting and teaching programs. There were endowments for new acquisitions. However, the city's fortunes began to decline in the mid-1970s, its major industry deeply affected by the energy crisis. Nevertheless, attendance continued to hold steady, and the museum maintained its ambitious exhibition schedule as well as its strong relationship with the university. Unfortunately, the museum was receiving only small gifts. The descendants of the museum's founders had either left the city or had no interest in the museum. There were no major donors left.

Former director Art Spencer had tried everything. He raised museum admission fees for out-of-towners, sadly without noticeable impact on the budget. He partnered actively with the university and every heritage institution in the city. He increased school visits to the museum and visited local schools himself. To his credit, he raised the institution's visibility. Then he encouraged the museum staff to apply for grants. The librarians and curators were successful in their applications. And the new head of development increased corporate sponsorships. But these initiatives were not enough: the endowment did not grow. The recession of 2008 hurt the museum as well.

The museum's portfolio was well diversified, and its losses were not as heavy as those at other museums. Still, because no major gifts were coming in, the museum could not seem to move forward. When Art Spencer turned sixty-five, he was ready to retire.

Enter the new director, Penny Hunt-Moore, who was eager to accept the museum's challenges head-on—and to make her mark. She entered the museum with the confidence of someone who had had a meteoric rise. Not yet forty, she had already served in key curatorial and administrative positions in several major museums. She was cosmopolitan and well connected. She had a PhD from one of the most prestigious art history programs in the country. It was widely predicted that in a few years she would become director of a major museum.

Within three months of her arrival, Hunt-Moore had a lucky break. She was contacted by someone who had never made a donation to the Jackman but offered to donate $75 million if it could match half the gift in two years and come up with an exciting naming opportunity. The donor had made a fortune on Wall Street, and his wife was CEO of a large company. Both were eager to become prominent philanthropists but faced stiff competition for that honor in New York City. Then the wife thought of the Jackman, which was near their summer compound. They had once attended a museum event and really enjoyed it. They believed that their gift could have a big impact on the museum. They first thought of funding an addition. However, Hunt-Moore immediately convened the board and brought in a consultant.

The board came up with several ideas, and Hunt-Moore presented them to the donors. The idea ultimately selected was to reopen the beautiful original entrance to the museum—which had been closed in the previous renovation in the 1960s—and expand it to include a state-of-the-art auditorium, restaurant, makerspace, and arts workshop. A space for outdoor concerts was included in the plan. The donors insisted that only "young and edgy" architecture firms should be invited to submit proposals. Reconfiguring some of the old space and adding a minimal amount of new space would make the museum more inviting and draw in new audiences.

This vision was the beginning of the end of the library, which was situated adjacent to what would become the new space. And there was no place else to locate it. The director, in the stated belief that most of the library collections could be found on the Internet, decided to move its books and journals to an off-site storage facility that would be shared with the university. The books could be paged if anyone wanted to use them. The archival assistant would be given a small office near the registrar. There was enough room in the museum basement to house the archives.

CONCLUSION

This case illustrates the challenges that libraries and archives face when there is a realignment of priorities and a shift in resource allocation. This museum decided to put all its newly acquired funding into something it viewed as more exciting than a library. New spaces attract new visitors, it reasoned. And one can only assume that the director hoped that this large gift would attract more such gifts—and that the donors themselves might give additional funds to the museum.

Could the librarians have done anything differently? Probably not; they had already contributed to the museum through their grants. The new director engaged only the trustees and the donors in the strategic planning; the museum staff did not participate. In fact, the librarians did not have a clue that such a decision was possible, let alone being made. In such a top-down environment, the librarians could have done little. Further, when the announcement was made that the library would close, no one—staff, scholars, museum curators, trustees, or the general public—fought the decision. This study shows that not even a successful unit—as the library was with its grant funding—is guaranteed survival.

* * *

Postscript: Georgina, once she got past her initial shock and incredulity, decided against filing a lawsuit and found a job as director of the fine arts library in a university in another city. Michaela became assistant director for public outreach at a large public library. She was philosophical and upbeat when we interviewed her for a second time. She told us that she had really enjoyed her years at the museum and felt that her grant-writing skills had made her competitive for the public library job—which she loves. "It is ironic," she observed, "that I could be doing public outreach in the museum's new makerspace. I guess the director did not understand that librarians don't only work behind the scenes."

Chapter Twelve

The American Textile History Museum, 1960–2018

A Museum That Lives On through Its Collections

Michèle V. Cloonan

Small, privately funded, nonprofit cultural heritage institutions face ongoing sustainability challenges. Such institutions may eventually close for some of the reasons presented in this chapter. This case study explores the closure of the American Textile History Museum (ATHM), focusing on challenges that the museum had faced for a long time. It highlights the many ways in which the museum tried to reverse its declining fortunes. Once its closure became inevitable, the museum undertook a painstaking process to best disperse its collections and remaining assets.

INTERVIEWS

For this case we interviewed curators, librarians, and administrators over a period of eight years. Interviews and meetings were conducted during the research funded by the Institute of Museum and Library Services, from 2009 to 2012, and our collaboration continued through 2018. We have drawn on interviews conducted by Simmons University students and faculty. Librarians Claire Sheridan and Jane Ward were particularly helpful. In addition, we drew on numerous published sources and web pages, including the *ATHM News* (http://www.athm.org/news), 2001–2017; Smithsonian Affiliations (https://affiliations.si.edu); and the University of Massachusetts, Lowell website (https://www.uml.edu).[1]

BACKGROUND AND HISTORY

The ATHM was founded in 1960 by Caroline Stevens Rogers (1894–1985) as the Merrimack Valley Textile Museum in North Andover, Massachusetts. Rogers, a hand-weaver and dyer, had inherited a collection of spinning wheels, hand looms, and related equipment and tools from her father, Samuel Dale Stevens (1859–1922), founder of the North Andover Historical Society and partner in M. T. Stevens & Sons Company (MTS & Co.). Her husband, Horatio Rogers, a retired physician, was responsible for restoring this collection, and Mrs. Rogers wanted to find a permanent home for it.

Her interest in the textile industry came naturally as she was the great-granddaughter of Moses Nathaniel Stevens, founder in 1813 of the Stevens Mill, North Andover's first woolen mill. Having enlarged its mill holdings, Stevens Mill was incorporated around 1890 as M. T. Stevens & Sons. In 1946, the family-owned business merged with J. P. Stevens & Company (JPS & Co.) of New York, its selling agent, which had expanded into the cotton industry. The parent firm of MTS & Co. became a subsidiary of JPS & Co. In 1988, JPS & Co. went out of business in a hostile takeover.

Caroline Rogers wanted to donate her collection to an institution that would use it to educate the public about the significance of textile manufacturing "by collecting, preserving and exhibiting objects of historical, antiquarian, artistic or technological interest . . . [by] publishing, and acquiring and maintaining books, records and other writings . . . and [by] acquiring, maintaining, exhibiting and publishing pictures, photographs, drawings and models of any and all kinds."[2]

Since the North Andover Historical Society did not have the space to display the Samuel Dale Stevens collection, in 1959 its board hired a professional historian, J. Bruce Sinclair, who recommended that Mrs. Rogers establish a separate museum that would be administered by its own staff and board, separate from the historical society. Sinclair became the museum's first director in May 1960. Land was leased from the historical society, and funds were raised to construct a building adjacent to the historical society, at 800 Massachusetts Avenue. The Merrimack Valley Textile Museum was incorporated in June 1960, and the building was completed in July 1961. The staff consisted of the director, a librarian, a part-time curator, and a secretary. Samuel Dale Stevens's collection of wooden tools and machinery formed the curatorial collections, and the extensive records of the companies that made up Stevens Mills became the nucleus of the library's manuscript collections. The first librarian, Rex Parady, built the collections with a small endowment. Parady traveled extensively to acquire appropriate materials, including early European materials relating to the textile industry and the Industrial Revolution.

In 1964, Thomas Leavitt replaced Sinclair as director. During his twenty-seven-year tenure the museum steadily expanded. In 1967, a six-thousand-foot library wing was added, and in 1970 the trustees voted to construct Machinery Hall, a thirty-thousand-square-foot storage facility, in North Andover to house tools and machinery. The museum's scope continued to expand to include the industry throughout the United States, primarily but not exclusively up to 1950, and all-natural fibers. In 1973 the museum was accredited by the American Alliance of Museums. Also in that year, the New England Conservation Center—now the Northeast Document Conservation Center (NEDCC)—was invited to lease space in the museum. NEDCC remained there until 1976, when it moved to Abbot Hall at Phillips Academy in Andover. After NEDCC moved, the Textile Conservation Center was established at the museum in 1977.[3] The library continued to expand, eventually acquiring the books and periodical collections of the Lowell Textile School (LTS), which was founded in 1895 to train technicians and managers for the textile industry. LTS merged in 1975 with the Lowell Normal School to form the University of Lowell, which closed its textile programs and transferred textile-related materials to the Merrimack Valley Textile Museum. The University of Lowell became part of the University of Massachusetts system in 1991.

In the 1980s, G. Gordon and Marjorie Osborne donated money to the library. He was the president and treasurer of the Warwick Mills from 1948 onward. The company manufactured parachute material during World War II and later manufactured DuPont's Kevlar® para-aramid fiber. The museum received a $1 million bequest from the Osbornes in 2013.

In 1984, the trustees decided that the name of the museum should reflect its expanding reach, and it became the Museum of American Textile History. At around the same time the museum expanded its scope further to include manmade and contemporary materials. The library and collections continued to grow. The space in North Andover was no longer adequate. Additionally, the board wanted to locate the museum somewhere with better public access and to incorporate all its collections under one roof. The trustees looked at several sites in Lawrence throughout the late 1980s and into the early 1990s, but these buildings were eventually rejected.

The museum finally found—and purchased—a suitable space, and in 1992 it moved from North Andover to Lowell, Massachusetts. The building was the five-story, 157,000-square-foot Kitson Machine Shop building, located at 491 Dutton Street in downtown Lowell. After the move, the museum changed its name again, this time to the American Textile History Museum, the name it would retain until its closure in 2018. According to the ATHM website,

> During its first thirty years, the Museum documented the woolen, cotton, flax and silk industries in New England and beyond through its collections of pre-industrial tools, powered industrial era machinery, flat textiles and the rich collections of its Osborne Library.
>
> The Museum supported research and publication, hosted conferences, presented exhibitions and public programming. It also developed a model program with the public schools of neighboring Lawrence, Massachusetts. In 1977, the Textile Conservation Center was established as a department of the Museum. [The lab was closed in 2006; see below.]
>
> By the mid-1980s, under the directorship of Tom Leavitt, the Museum set out to expand its public dimension via exhibitions and expanded museum educational programming for schools and the general public. It also sought to bring its extensive collections into a single, unified curatorial and storage facility.
>
> In 1992, the Museum purchased the Kitson Building in Lowell and began a fundraising campaign, to support the renovations to this historic building. Led by Director Paul Rivard, the building was renovated, the core exhibition Textiles in America was designed and installed, and the Museum opened to the public in April 1997. Under Rivard's guidance, the Museum expanded its educational services to include the Lowell Public Schools and initiated the special changing exhibitions program.[4]

Over the next twenty years, the museum continued to expand its scope and programs but was ultimately unable to sustain its business model, despite fund-raising efforts, cost-cutting measures, and revenue-generating initiatives. Funds to operate the museum were taken from the endowment, which steadily decreased.[5] The following is a synopsis of activities from 2000 through the ATHM's 2018 closure.

2000–2005

Under director Michael J. Smith, the museum created a new mission statement, expanded its educational programs, including programs for Scouts and a Textile Learning Center for families, and established the American Textile Hall of Fame, a program to honor people, corporations, and organizations associated with the textile industry. The museum received funding from the Malcolm and Elizabeth Chace Foundation to provide Internet access to its collections.

2006–2011

James S. Coleman became director. He was the first of three directors who would oversee the museum through its financial crisis and eventual closure. The process of closing the Textile Conservation Center and the sale of half the building to the *Lowell Sun* newspaper and a condominium developer had been initiated before Coleman's arrival; Coleman finalized the process. He focused on improving the visibility of the museum, cost cutting, and fund-raising. The "Campaign for the American Textile History Museum," launched in 2006, succeeded in reaching its goal to raise $1.5 million to fund the museum's renovation, $1 million for its endowment, and $1.4 million for operating costs. However, the museum continued to operate at a deficit. In 1997, the museum had nearly fifty full- and part-time staff. By the time Coleman left, it had fourteen.

In an interview conducted by Simmons University students, Coleman described the Osborne Library as "the foremost asset of the collection in the museum as it's known in the Americas . . . and possibly the world."[6] Other accomplishments during Coleman's tenure include the following:

- The Chace Catalogue, funded by Malcolm and Elizabeth Chace and the Chace Foundation, came online in June 2006, enabling visitors to gain online access to key portions of ATHM's curatorial and storage facilities through the technology of a virtual museum. (The catalog didn't include all collection information. For example, an early version of the MIMSY collection management system was used for cataloging the collections. By 2012, there were seventy-two thousand records in MIMSY and thirty-two thousand in the Chace Catalogue.) The library contributed records to OCLC until its closure.
- In 2008, ATHM created a mascot, Lulu the Lamb.
- After renovations, the museum reopened in 2009 with a new permanent exhibit, "Textile Revolution: An Exploration through Space and Time."
- ATHM became a member of Smithsonian Affiliations the same year. As described on the Smithsonian website, "Smithsonian Affiliations is a division of the Smithsonian Institution that establishes long-term partnerships with non-Smithsonian museums and educational and cultural organizations, in order to share collections, exhibitions and educational strategies and conduct joint research. Partner organizations are known as 'Smithsonian Affiliates' and are allowed to use the tag line 'In Association with the Smithsonian Institution' and the approved Smithsonian Affiliations logo on their website, programming, and marketing material. Any 501(c)3 non-profit or publicly operated educational entity can apply to become a Smithsonian Affiliate."[7]

2011–2015

In November 2011, Jonathan Stevens was hired as interim director. A member of the Stevens textile-manufacturing family, he had previously served on the ATHM Board of Trustees. He was named president and CEO in March 2012 and remained in charge through the summer of 2015. During his tenure, further efforts were made to stabilize the museum, but it continued to operate at a deficit.

2015–2018

In September 2015, Todd Smith became interim director. Smith had previously been director of institutional advancement and was asked to step in as director. According to the ATHM website, "On November 3, 2015, the ATHM Board of Trustees voted to undergo a dramatic transformation for ATHM, seeking strategic partnerships and major fundraising to preserve and protect ATHM's core collection and enable the Museum to fulfill its mission for generations to come. The Museum's exhibits and galleries temporarily closed to the public in early 2016 to enable the Museum to focus on the transformation."

The museum explored a possible merger with the Lowell National Historical Park.

> For more than eight months, ATHM engaged with Nonprofit Finance Fund and Laura Roberts Consulting for strategic evaluation and business planning, seeking to identify and explore all reasonable options available to the Museum, including downsizing, restructuring, and merging with another organization. ATHM identified a strategic partnership with the Lowell National Historical Park as the alternative with the best potential for fiscal and operational viability. The Park was very receptive to a partnership, and over a seven-month period, ATHM evaluated the financial and operational feasibility of more than a dozen LNHP partnership business models. However, no viable or sustainable business model with a meaningful scope of mission could be identified.[8]

No such partnership materialized. On May 24, 2016, the ATHM Board of Trustees voted to seek approval from the Massachusetts Attorney General's Office and Supreme Judicial Court to dissolve the museum's 501(c)(3) and permanently close its doors. ATHM board chair Matthew Coggins said, "This was an extremely difficult decision for all involved and certainly not the outcome we had hoped and worked for. . . . However, the Board recognizes that serious operational challenges, financial shortfalls, and other circumstances make it impossible to ethically and responsibly dedicate further financial assets to attempt to keep our doors open."[9]

PRESERVING THE COLLECTION

With the decision to close, the museum shifted its focus to protecting and preserving its historic and priceless collection and seeking to identify and execute the deaccessioning and transfer of its textile, library, and machinery collections to other nonprofit or government institutions for long-term stewardship, ongoing access, and contribution to the greater public benefit.

The primary focus of ATHM leadership—in close consultation with the Massachusetts Attorney General's Office—was to preserve the integrity of the core collections, transferring them in their entirety or with the largest portions intact. Over an eighteen-month period, the museum's leadership, staff, and Collections Committee—working collaboratively across its curatorial, library, and archives units—engaged in discussions with dozens of museums, libraries, educational institutions, and other nonprofits, successfully identifying and transferring over 95 percent of the museum's collections to more than one hundred committed organizations to serve as long-term stewards. In the end, 136 institutions received items from the collection. Many items were relocated to collections with links to their origins: for instance, the spinning wheel believed to have come from the Louisa May Alcott home is now housed at the Alcott's Orchard House in Concord, Massachusetts; the textile sample "Peace," woven by Auburn University Textile School students, is now housed at the Auburn University Libraries in Auburn, Alabama; and the oil painting *Middlesex Company Woolen Mill, Lowell, Mass.* is now at the Cape Ann Museum in Gloucester, Massachusetts. Most of the Osborne Library went to Cornell University Library in New York. A significant cross section of the museum's core costume collections was transferred to the Henry Ford Museum in Michigan. The bulk of the machinery collection went to Randolph Heritage Conservancy in North Carolina.

In early 2018, the museum completed the transfer of its collections.[10] During the summer of that year, the ATHM Board of Trustees filed for dissolution with the Massachusetts Supreme Judicial Court, and the American Textile History Museum ceased to exist.

CONCLUSION

For the final twenty years of its existence, ATHM could not keep pace with its operational costs nor establish a sizable endowment. Although its resources declined, its ambitions never did. Without sizable endowments, however, small, private museums like ATHM find it difficult, or even impossible, to survive. Of particular relevance for this book is that in the face of the ATHM closure, the museum had a dedicated staff who worked collaboratively in its deaccession and transfer efforts to find suitable homes for ATHM's rich collections. As a result, many cultural heritage institutions throughout the United States are the beneficiaries. The American Textile History Museum has closed, but its collections will live on.

The ATHM institutional archives will be processed by graduate students in the archives program at Simmons. Once processed, they will be turned over to the University of Massachusetts, Lowell. This is the final chapter in what has been a rich collaboration with ATHM.

NOTES

1. I am grateful for help from many members of the ATHM community, some of whom preferred to not be acknowledged by name.
2. "Minutes of Directors Meeting of the North Andover Historical Society," 1959 (excerpt).
3. American Textile History Museum, accessed July 23, 2018, http://www.athm.org. The website will be maintained through 2018; "Who We Are/What We Do," Northeast Document Conservation Center, accessed July 23, 2018, https://www.nedcc.org/about/overview.
4. American Textile History Museum, accessed July 23, 2018, http://www.athm.org. The website will be maintained through 2018.
5. ATHM, IRS 990 forms, 2005–2015.
6. Based on interview transcripts from April 30, 2010, and October 14, 2011, with: Jeannette Bastian, Ross Harvey, Martha Mahard, and Terry Plum. Interviews with Diane Fagan Affleck, Clare Sheridan, and Jim Coleman, April 30, 2010; Caitlin Christian-Lamb, Ana Knezevic, and Margaret Rosequist. Interviews at ATHM with Clare Sheridan, James Coleman, and Kathy Hirbour, October 14, 2011.
7. Smithsonian Affiliations, accessed August 6, 2018, https://affiliations.si.edu.
8. "ATHM Seeks to Close Permanently," ATHM, accessed August 8, 2018, http://www.athm.org/news/athm-seeks-to-close.
9. "ATHM Seeks to Close Permanently."
10. The list of recipients was published at "New Homes of ATHM Collections," ATHM, accessed September 26, 2018, http://www.athm.org/about-athm/path-to-closure/athm-collections-transfer-update/future-homes-of-athm-collections.

Chapter Thirteen

Phillips Library, Peabody Essex Museum

Divergent Visions

Michèle V. Cloonan and Martha R. Mahard

This case study explores what happens when the interests of a museum library are seen to diverge from those of the museum it is part of. In this case, the museum used a library director's retirement as an opportunity to downsize the library staff and to move the collection nearly twenty miles from the museum. Two aspects of this case stand out: the museum director's twenty-year effort to downscale and diminish the library and the local community's efforts to keep the library in Salem, Massachusetts. This case offers a striking contrast to that of New York's Museum of Modern Art, where the interests of the library, archives, and museum are well aligned.

INTERVIEWS

The information for this case was gathered from current and former employees of the museum, community members, and people who attended the Salem community forums. The Phillips Library was a partner in the 2009 Institute of Museum and Library Services grant project, along with Historic New England, the American Textile History Museum, and several other cultural heritage organizations in New England.[1] Interviews conducted by the grant team and participating students provided useful information about the history of the library and the museum. Additional information was gleaned from the museum's website and the press.

BACKGROUND

The fate of a library—or, for that matter, any entity in a larger organization—depends on the institution's leadership and its understanding of the library's value within the institution. Museum libraries, however distinguished and valued they may be in the outside research community, often have only a tenuous hold on their place in the museum organization. Though research in its collections is a major part of the work conducted in a museum, few boards of trustees or administrators understand that the value and support of the library contributes directly to the museum's accomplishment of its mission and enhances its reputation. Most museum libraries exist to support the research in the collection by curators and the research community at large. Often museum libraries have amassed collections that are as rich and valuable as those at some of the top academic research libraries in the country.

Recently our attention was called to an old established museum (not the Phillips Library at the Peabody Essex Museum) with an equally old and established library collection. A museum director, after sweeping the room with a glance, declared that since all of this "stuff" was available online, there really was no need to maintain the library at all. In that instance, the director wanted to use the space occupied by the library for galleries for a newly acquired collection. The library was vulnerable because it occupied a prime spot in the building and could not be seen as part of the museum's revenue stream.

For a library to succeed in its larger setting, it must align with the museum's mission and vision. Some organizations now see the museum library as peripheral—no matter how much the library director may advocate for it.

At Harvard University, the Fine Arts Library is one of several branches of the Harvard College Library. For more than fifty years the library rented space in the building of the university's Fogg Art Museum. Indeed, in the early 1990s, a named reading room for the library was included in the Werner Otto Hall addition to the original Fogg building. When preparations and planning for the complete gutting of the Fogg and the demolition of Otto Hall were well advanced, the library learned that, contrary to expectations, the new museum building would not include housing for the library. The library, with its collection of books, photographs, slides, periodicals, and special collections, was forced to relocate on short notice. Because the library and its host museum were parts of the same parent institution, the museum did not lose the services of the library or access to its collections. But the move came at tremendous cost to the library and was a chilling demonstration of the low regard in which the library was held by the museum administration (and the university around it) at the time. While the museum spent nearly a decade raising funds and preparing to move the collection to a swing space for the construction period, the library had less than a year's notice and was expected to be back up and running in a matter of months. Clearly, at some level of the university, the museum and the library were not seen as aligned.

In other instances, where the museum library has been physically alienated from the museum's main building, we have seen the weakening of the library's position and a falling off of support. Few curators will walk or drive to another location, preferring instead to rely on their own departmental subcollections and, of course, the Internet.

Museum directors are most likely to have a specific agenda that they wish to accomplish—perhaps to enhance the museum's reputation through splendid new acquisitions or to garner fame through the addition of a new wing. Some directors may aim to take the museum in a completely new direction, away from its historic roots and to a different level of recognition in the museum world. In single-minded pursuit of such goals, the day-to-day functioning of the institution can get lost. Or a director may fail to understand how libraries can enhance exhibitions, education, or other forms of museum engagement with the public. Library directors may not realize that it is necessary to market their services to the rest of the museum. At one institution we studied, on the arrival of a new museum director, the longtime librarian told us that she planned to "lie low" so that the library might avoid cuts. But perhaps she should have done just the opposite—invited the new director to the library so that she could show him its treasures as well as its value to the museum.

The library in a museum in which it is undervalued—for whatever reason—is vulnerable. Funds directed to support the library may be jealously coveted for other priorities closer to the administration's vision and could be diverted from their original purposes in support of the library to aid the museum in its other pursuits.

HISTORY OF THE PHILLIPS LIBRARY

A case in point is the Phillips Library at the Peabody Essex Museum (PEM). The organization as it exists today has come a long way from its historical founding collections. Shifting away from local and maritime history, East Asian collections, natural history, and ethnological specimens, the museum today presents itself first as a museum of art and culture. The library, made up of important individual collections from several institutions that merged over time, continues to reflect the collecting interests and strengths of the founders as they were developed for more than two centuries. Lost on the senior administrators is the fact that the invaluable collections could be fully supporting the museum's research and exhibitions programs and actually do support the work of innumerable scholars worldwide.

When founded in 1799, the East India Marine Society was what, in its day, was called a "cabinet of curiosity"—a structure that eventually would become a museum. Its founders were wealthy shipowners and ship captains whose mission, among other things, was to bring back treasures to Salem, where the society was born. To be a member of the society, one had to have sailed beyond the Cape of Good Hope or Cape Horn. The museum's holdings were objects from all over the world—from wherever the founders' ships sailed, which included the Far East, Africa, and the Pacific Ocean, among other places. The founders were well educated, so they also had their own individual libraries, which, when merged at the museum's founding, became a substantial research collection covering all the subjects represented by the objects in the museum in considerable depth. Hence, every kind of object that the society held had a wealth of literature associated with it—printed books and pamphlets and manuscript materials of various kinds—and, later on, photographs by the hundreds of thousands.

In about 1869, the East India Marine Society changed its name to the Peabody Academy of Science. And in the early twentieth century, the institution's name became the Peabody Museum of Salem. As the museum grew and embraced new areas, so did its library.

In 1821 the Essex Historical Society was founded, with its primary focus on—of course—Essex County, its history and growth. And in 1833 the Essex County Natural History Society was founded, with a similar mission. These two organizations merged in 1848 to become the Essex Institute. Again, the organization, like the East India Marine Society, was more than merely a local historical society; it was a museum with its own substantial library and history, representing Essex County culture in all its manifestations. The complex chain of transfers and mergers is explained on the Peabody Essex Museum's website:

> In the late 1860s, the Essex Institute refined its mission to the collection and presentation of regional art, history and architecture. In so doing, it transferred its natural history and archaeology collections to the East India Marine Society's descendent organization, the Peabody Academy of Science (the "Peabody"). In turn, the Peabody, renamed for its great benefactor, the philanthropist George Peabody, transferred its historical collections to the Essex. . . .
>
> With their physical proximity, closely connected boards and overlapping collections, the possibility of consolidating the Essex and the Peabody had been discussed over the years.
>
> After in-depth studies showed the benefits of such a merger, the consolidation of these two organizations into the new PEM was effected in July 1992. The museum possessed extraordinary collections—more than 840,000 works of art and culture featuring maritime art and history; American art; Asian, Oceanic, and African art; Asian export art; two large libraries with over 400,000 books, manuscripts, and documents; and 22 historic buildings.[2]

Each organization had a Phillips Library, so after the 1992 merger, the new museum simply kept the name Phillips Library, with many treasures and a broad and rich collection covering all the areas of the museum's object history. The Phillips Library is among the top-five art museum libraries in the United States in holdings and quality. Its collection is exceptionally rich in many areas, including East Asian (China, Japan, Korea, and India), Pacific Rim, Native American, and African art, American decorative arts, maritime subjects, local history, furniture and architecture, and much more. Because the original collecting was so specifically focused, the collection has a far greater depth and breadth than many research institutions with similar collecting interests.

To facilitate the 1992 merger, the museum brought in a new director with a track record in museum management but no apparent interest in or experience with libraries. He understood museum operations and had a vision of converting PEM into a "museum of art and culture," forsaking the institution's historical roots. No longer would the museum focus broadly on horticulture, ethnography, medicine, genealogy, or any of the natural sciences. The library collection, then, would be newly focused on art and culture, and the older, rich, and broad collections outside that focus would merely sit on the shelves, not featured in any kind of outreach.

Scholars, however, knowing of the library's great strengths, kept showing up to do research in these older collecting areas, and to this day the library supports publications in many fields beyond "art and culture." It is telling, however, how the museum's leadership has shaped the fate of the library. In 2004, the museum cut the staff and library hours (see below under "Staffing"). Objections to these cuts on the part of the public and some of the trustees led to the hiring of a new library director in 2007. Soon after being hired, he was called into the museum director's office. The museum director told the librarian, "I once had to work under a librarian and I hated it." At a meeting of the trustees soon after, the museum director suggested transferring the library to Salem State University. He quickly withdrew the proposal when one trustee spoke up against this. The director's second in command constantly rejected one suggestion after another from the librarian about kinds of outreach that the library could do for itself, for the institution as a whole, and for the public. The museum director's old enmity for libraries would not go away.

With the assistance of the museum's development office, the library was encouraged to seek a substantial grant to hold two symposia at PEM concerning art museum libraries. The library obtained funding from outside organizations, including the Institute of Museum and Library Services, and successfully hosted two well-received symposia (in 2010 and 2012). To the museum's honor, it did a superb job of hosting the over three hundred attendees at these two events. Yet, despite the success of the symposia, the museum's senior administration couldn't see how PEM could benefit by advancing its own library and archives.

When he was first hired in 2007, the library director was not a member of the museum's Executive Leadership Team. Although discouraged by his immediate supervisor, he petitioned to join the team, and the museum director agreed. He was nevertheless warned by his supervisor not to use the meetings to advocate for the library as the meetings were strictly for the discussion of museum business. Though he had succeeded in getting a place at the table, the library was not much advanced by his forced silence. He persisted in his efforts to reach out to trustees and donors, hosting tours of the library and show-and-tell sessions. These efforts led to the Phillips Library's being given its first opportunity in over two hundred years to have an exhibition solely devoted to library treasures. Because he had direct access to the trustees and other donors, the library director was able to raise money specifically for certain features of the exhibition. Although the library raised the money for its own exhibition, the special features were not installed, and the museum kept the money for other uses.

Problems with access to funds for the library continued and worsened over time. Staffing levels, public access to the collections, and acquisitions were all adversely affected.

STAFFING

At the merger of the two institutions in 1992, there were fourteen librarians in the Phillips Library. Within a decade there were three. When the new library director was hired in 2007, the library, with its treasures and great scholarly resources, was open to the public on Tuesdays from 1 p.m. to 4 p.m. and Thursdays from 10 a.m. to 4 p.m. Scholars complained about the curtailed hours—not merely that there were no weekend or evening hours. The library was seriously understaffed, and opening for additional hours was not an option. The new library director asked to increase the hours, beginning only modestly: opening the reading room on Tuesdays from 10 a.m. to 4 p.m. (as was done on Thursdays). He was denied this. He said that the staff (which by the time he was hired was up to four full-time employees) was already onsite for those extra hours. The security guards were already in place then as well. There was essentially no fiscal impact whatsoever to opening to the public for those extra three hours. Again, he was denied. No reason was given. But the library was clearly being "underemphasized" as part of the museum director's aim of controlling it.

ACCESS TO THE COLLECTIONS

Museums are chronically in need of new revenue streams and constantly seek new ways to further monetize collections, including the always controversial move to deaccession parts of the collection. While departmental entrepreneurship may be encouraged, it is seldom rewarded. The library director secured funds for the library by contracting with a vendor to digitize an important collection and then receiving a royalty for the sale of those images. When the royalty came in, it was absorbed into funds selected by the museum director's deputy; the library, led to believe the profits would accrue to it, never saw any of the money. In another instance a trustee, whose foundation gave yearly to the museum and who loved the library presentations, became an enthusiastic member of its visiting committee (a friends-of-the-library group). After being on the committee for a few years, he made a generous gift specifically to the library. The library director was copied on a letter with this designation of the foundation's year-end gift. Early the following year the library director learned that not a penny of it had gone to the library—it all went to the museum. When the library director asked about it, he was told that the museum needed the money more than the library did. He was assured that what the museum had done was perfectly legitimate since the funds went "to offset library expenses."

This is not an uncommon practice in the not-for-profit sector. Endowed funds must be carefully worded to ensure that they are used for the purpose intended by the donor. General language that only specifies that the money be used in support of the library can be interpreted broadly and the money diverted to a variety of managerial purposes including payroll, upkeep, preservation, and other less visible costs unlikely to have been envisaged by the original donor. Wording a bequest specifically for the purchase or preservation of books and manuscripts can do away with this problem—but not always.

ACQUISITION FUNDS

When hired in 2007, the library director had control of a large number of endowed funds for the purchase of rare books and other research materials. Some of the funds were well over one hundred years old. They were generating something in the neighborhood of $200,000 a year and were clearly designated library funds, mostly for acquisitions in specified areas (e.g., books and maps about Essex County, Canadiana, books on maritime issues, and so forth) or for conservation or outreach. At one point, however, the library director's supervisor decided to "reinterpret" these endowed funds, and overnight the available funds for acquisition were reduced by about 85 percent. Without staff and without funds for ongoing acquisitions to maintain the collection, the library has been severely diminished.

The library director fought on but was repeatedly thwarted as funds raised for the benefit of the library were appropriated for use by the museum. His efforts to secure funding to keep the library functioning at an acceptable level were ultimately to little avail.

Today, the library has been absorbed into the organizational structure of the museum in such a way as to put it on a level with other collecting departments, overseen by a museum collections officer, and with no commitment to outreach and research. Despite the fact that the library directorship was a named, endowed position, the Ann C. Pingree Library Directorship, the management of the museum has chosen not to replace the retired librarian but instead to combine the position with that of the chief of collections services. Hence the Ann C. Pingree Library Director is no longer a librarian. The actual collection of rare materials has essentially ground to a halt. The library is no longer seen as a fine rare book collection and is now merely one of the museum's many collections.

As mentioned at the outset of this case study, an institution's leadership makes decisions based on its own vision and desire to shape the future of the institution. PEM's leadership may be able to justify its decisions with the claim that financial exigency, logic, and superior management of the collections have guided their choices. They may maintain that the museum and the library are one large institution with the same goals: to satisfy their trustees and serve their public. But this was not a typical museum/library situation. This library was never singularly designed to serve an art and culture museum and its curators. The library has existed for more than two hundred years as a research entity serving thousands beyond the museum's leaders and patrons and in areas far beyond the museum's current collecting interests. It has had a life of its own, as a research facility, despite its close ties to the larger institution. In character it is much closer to independent research libraries such as the Folger Shakespeare Library, the Massachusetts Historical Society, or the American Antiquarian Society. It is this aspect that the museum management seems to find most antithetical to its purposes as it continues to try to trim the library into a shape for which it was never intended.

The Phillips Library collections are amazing in breadth and depth, with world-class holdings in many collecting areas and with great untapped potential. But that potential will not be met under the present leadership. And given the recent decision to move the Phillips Library to a warehouse that is sixteen miles away from the main museum, it is unlikely that a future director will be able to undo the damage that has been done. Whether this was a deliberate downsizing move or not, the end result is that the vital and once heavily used Phillips Library is now languishing, essentially rudderless as a library; its once vital collections program has been eviscerated and its future as a venue for scholarship and research called into question. The museum director has essentially hidden the collection many miles away from the museum. A library needs to be public facing and accessible to provide the best information and research services.

Despite vigorous community outcry, the museum decided that the historic buildings that formerly held the Phillips Library will be renovated, not to house the library's collections as originally planned but to serve as museum offices.[3] The end result is that the once heavily used Phillips Library may languish, hidden from the museum and all but unavailable for research.

Museum administrations need to be held accountable for decisions that involve endowments and major capital donations. Yet, in many ways, their operations remain the least transparent of any in the not-for-profit world, as this case and our anonymous case show.

CONCLUSION

Over the last few decades, organizations have come to understand that working in isolation—in what have metaphorically been called "silos"—is costly in more ways than one. Libraries, archives, and museums have a great deal in common, with overlapping staffing issues, clientele, and operational responsibilities and practices. They have recognized that when they combine their resources and work together, they can accomplish much more than each individual institution can accomplish on its own. The Metropolitan Museum of Art has a splendid library and a superb archive, and the units collaborate in their public programs and in researching, creating, and presenting exhibitions. The chief of archive, library, and research collections at the Museum of Modern Art, Michelle Elligott, has successfully integrated the archives into the life of the museum, as is also described in this volume. An isolationist structure, with a museum operating as if it has no library (when a great one is at hand—under its "own roof") and no archives, is costly, narrow-minded, and ultimately a disservice to the community it is intended to serve.

Postscript: As we went to press, the museum has posted a head librarian position. To reinforce the demotion of the library, the posting made clear that the library head would work under the Ann C. Pingree Library Director, who is not a librarian. This reinforces the idea that the library is now seen as merely one of the museum's collections, like its paintings, sculptures, and textiles, instead of as a unit that supports the entire museum. To its credit, PEM recognizes that the library needs someone with library experience to run it. It looks as if the (unsuccessful) public outcry to keep the library in

Salem, near the museum, has shown PEM's leadership that it does need a trained librarian overseeing this venerable collection.

NOTES

1. IMLS Grant, Laura Bush 21st Century Librarian Program, RE-05-09-0082-09. "Curriculum, Cooperation, Convergence, Capacity: 4Cs for the Development of Cultural Heritage Institutions: Libraries, Museums, and Archives in the Twenty-First Century," 2009–2012, accessed August 11, 2018, https://www.imls.gov/grants/awarded/re-05-09-0082-09.

2. "About PEM. Museum History," Peabody Essex Museum, accessed June 28, 2018, https://www.pem.org/about-pem/museum-history.

3. For examples of the Salem community's outcry, see Malcolm Gay, "Salem Residents Angry over Museum's Plan to Move Historical Records," *Boston Globe*, accessed January 13, 2018, http://www.bostonglobe.com/arts/art/2018/01/12/salem-residents-angry-over-museum-plan-move-historical-records/8k6firnLfZVG1weLTVciFO/story.html; dasegar, "An Open Letter to Leadership of the Peabody Essex Museum," *streetsofsalem* (blog), December 18, 2017, accessed June 15, 2018, https://streetsofsalem.com/2017/12/18/an-open-letter-to-the-leadership-of-the-peabody-essex-museum.

Part V

Culturally Sensitive Materials

Chapter Fourteen

The Peabody Museum of Archaeology and Ethnology at Harvard University

The Value of Digitizing Museum Archives

Peter Botticelli

The Peabody Museum of Archaeology and Ethnology at Harvard University was founded in 1866 with a gift from financier and philanthropist George Peabody (1795–1869). The museum, now part of the Harvard Museums of Science and Culture consortium, is responsible for one of the world's oldest and largest ethnological collections, with 1.6 million objects and extensive archival collections, including five hundred thousand photographs. We found the Peabody to be an intriguing case of a museum with great potential to expand its user base through digitization and online access, as reflected by the current strategic plan for the museum's Collections Division, which emphasizes innovation and digital initiatives by the Archives, Collections Management, Conservation, and Registration departments. The Peabody is firmly committed to public access to its collections, and yet the institution also recognizes that it carries a heavy burden of stewardship for the huge volume of culturally sensitive information in the museum. This is a challenge the Peabody shares with the many museums whose collections have been acquired through the work of archaeologists and anthropologists who, beginning in the nineteenth century, made it a routine practice to collect and thus to relocate objects from their places of origin and to recontextualize objects within museum collections that often represent cultures (e.g., Europe and the United States) other than those that were responsible for creating and using objects before the arrival of scholar-collectors from institutions such as Harvard.

INTERVIEWS

We initially approached the Peabody with the general question of how libraries, archives, and museums (LAMs) are handling the ethics of digitization and online access to culturally sensitive materials. Yet, as we looked deeper, we also became intrigued by the current and potential role of the Peabody archives, a vital source of documentation for the museum collection that also provides a critical source of evidence on the development of anthropology as an academic discipline beginning in the 1800s. In this context, recent efforts to digitize the Peabody archives, particularly its photograph collections, offer valuable insights into how digital access could raise the visibility of museum archives, both as a source of evidence about how and why the museum collection was acquired and as a stand-alone cultural heritage resource. To learn more about the digitization of the Peabody archives, we interviewed three members of the archives staff: Patricia Kervick, senior archivist; Katherine Satriano, associate archivist; and Kim Allegretto, assistant archivist.[1]

HISTORY

From its earliest days, the Peabody sponsored many research expeditions and has long played a dynamic role as a center for research and study within Harvard University. Fieldwork by Harvard ethnographers has resulted in particularly strong collections representing the indigenous cultures of North, Central, and South America. The Peabody has significant Native American collections dating as far back as the early 1800s and one of the world's most valuable and extensive collections of Mesoamerican artifacts. Harvard ethnographers also conducted many expeditions to the Pacific islands, resulting in valuable collections for a number of cultures in that region. Africa, Asia, and Europe are also well represented in the museum, making the Peabody's collections truly global in scope.[2] The museum's eight public galleries can display only a small fraction of the collections, making digitization and online access an important strategic goal, as the museum "strives to make collections widely accessible" even as its collections raise complex issues for digital access, especially as the Peabody also plays "an active part in the history of American anthropology and in the evolving relationship between museums and native peoples."[3] As we will see below, digitization has the potential to advance, or perhaps to complicate, the ongoing dialogue between museums and indigenous cultures by making previously inaccessible objects and archival records discoverable online. By expanding access to all facets of the museum—collected objects and associated records—digitization has a great potential to advance scholarship by illuminating the complex histories of LAMs as they have gone about collecting and interpreting cultural heritage.

DIGITIZATION

To date, the Peabody has roughly a half million digital images available online, a figure that includes about two hundred thousand representing archives. Digitization efforts at the museum have largely coincided with the development of a formal archives program, as the Peabody hired its first full-time archivist in 1996. An important step came in 2002, when the archives was made responsible for both paper records and photographs. Starting in 2000, the Harvard Library Digital Initiative led to the digitization of forty thousand photographs (dating from the 1920s through the 1950s) in the archives' Carnegie Institute of Washington Central America Collection. In 2006, the Peabody archives received the first of two National Endowment for the Humanities grants (which ran through 2012) to digitize the seventy thousand photographic negatives in the collection; this was the first large-scale digitization project managed directly by the archives staff. In 2013 and 2014, the Collections Department digitized the museum's accession files as a key source of metadata needed to support online access. As part of this effort, the archives acquired a large volume of records not related to collections management or registration, including field notes donated by researchers over the years.

The archives has prioritized photographs and photographic negatives for digitization because of preservation concerns around the stable yet fragile state of the originals, a factor complicated by researchers' relatively high demand for these materials both in material form and through digital surrogates made available through Collections Online, the Peabody's web portal. For archaeologists, the photographs offer an essential means to document the condition of objects and sites as they are found and to chart their deterioration over time. Given the high research value of the photograph collection, in 2013 the Peabody decided to digitize its Historic Boards ("H boards") collection, which consists of nearly three hundred boxes of mat boards mounted in the late nineteenth and early twentieth centuries with one or more photographs, likely for educational use in classes at Harvard. To capture the full range of information values contained in the H boards, the Peabody decided to create a series of digital images for each board, including one capturing the whole board at a resolution that renders the caption easily readable, an image of the back of the board (if it contains relevant information), and a separate image of each photograph as it appeared before being mounted on the board.

Many of the H boards have handwritten captions describing the subject matter and often the location depicted in the photographs. About a quarter of the H boards can be linked directly to the museum's collections by the presence of an accession number written on the board; this signifies that the photograph was formally given to the museum by a donor. Those that do not have an accession number have been collected in a less formal manner, as ancillary material, such as expedition field notes, or as a stand-alone photograph collection treated differently than other object types. For the many H boards with no accession number, research by staff members can often establish a link to collection objects or other archival records, but staff time for this purpose is limited. Otherwise, not much is known about the history or original purpose of the H boards, especially as the collection was never formally appraised or processed by current archival standards. The H boards are mentioned in the 1915 Peabody annual report: "The Museum's collection of photographs now numbers approximately 15,000. These are being mounted on cards of uniform size, classified and arranged by Miss Gleason, in a specially designed cabinet file, the first section of which has been completed."[4] Clearly the photographs document the work of Harvard ethnographers, and intellectually they serve as a natural extension of the Peabody's collecting role and its educational mission within the university.

By digitizing the H boards, the archives have exposed many high-quality, individual images. The digital surrogates also reveal important information about the way the photographs were combined and given captions, written on the boards, over a century ago. It is also important that the H boards came to be stored in a way that added significant value for researchers—for instance, by being placed in boxes labeled simply by geography alone. Perhaps by accident, this minimalist way of classifying the H boards made it very convenient to search the collection according to particular countries or cultures, even in the absence of a finding aid for the collection as a whole. Once a search is narrowed to a geographic area, flipping through boxes of H boards—viewing the captions along with the attached photographs—has proven an efficient and popular way to find visual information. As Patricia Kervick notes, the H boards are the "first group of photographs that we search when receiving a photo request that is not from a specific collection. Often researchers request things by subject matter (e.g., 'man with tattoo') rather than from a specific accession," and as long as searches can be narrowed down to particular geographic areas, relevant results can often be obtained quickly.

For example, one H board (2004.29.24259.1) provides a detailed photograph of a man with a leg tattoo. The mat board was originally inscribed with a minimum of contextual information: the location (the Marquesas Islands) and the provenance ("Woodworth 1898")—just enough information for the archivists to link the photograph to the records of William McMichael Woodworth, a Harvard zoologist who collected over two hundred photographs of Oceania while visiting the region with other Harvard faculty in the late 1800s. This photograph could be highly useful to a researcher interested in Marquesan or, more broadly, Polynesian tattoos, and it would likely stand out to an archivist searching through boxes of H boards from this geographic region. Through the digitization process, the archivists were able to provide further context to users by labeling the photograph "Studio portrait of a man with tattooed leg," indicating that the photograph provides visual information not just about Marquesan tattoos but also about how a Marquesan from this era posed intentionally for a photograph that clearly highlights a leg tattoo. As they have been digitized, the H boards serve as a fine illustration of how particular items can operate across the conceptual boundaries separating a library geared to subject-based searches and information, a museum that curates rare or unique objects with scientific or aesthetic value, and an archives that is charged with preserving evidence of a creator's activities and intentions.

ONLINE ACCESS

From an archival perspective, the digitized H boards combine multiple layers of evidence, highlighting the subject matter of the photographs as they were taken originally and the ways in which museum staff later interpreted them as they were arranged and described on the mat boards. At all levels, we can point to many H boards that include culturally sensitive content, which in some cases calls for access restrictions in the Collections Online portal. In fact, the museum has a formal web security process in which all images are reviewed at the item level before they may appear online. The review process is guided by a detailed access policy that seeks to address the many cultural nuances that might come into play as an image is viewed by different audiences, including researchers, the general public, and those who might see it as a reflection of their culture. Once an image and associated metadata are reviewed by museum staff, a web security code is entered in the collections management system. In most cases, items will be coded for full open access for metadata and images. Still, the museum plans to update its software so that an advisory notice will precede the display of certain open access items to enable users to forgo viewing images with potentially sensitive content. In cases calling for access restrictions, staff are now able to limit the display of items to metadata only, while in some cases images may be visible to users who have registered and been approved by staff beforehand.

In setting its online access policies, the Native American Graves Protection and Repatriation Act (NAGPRA) has been an important factor for the Peabody, even though this 1990 U.S. federal law predates the rise of the web. It was originally designed to facilitate the repatriation of culturally sensitive artifacts, including human remains and funerary objects. Under NAGPRA, federally recognized American Indian tribes and Native Hawaiian organizations may assign representatives who can make formal requests for the repatriation of collection objects. Using this framework, the Peabody's online access policy is designed to give NAGPRA representatives access to sensitive items while at the same time limiting access to images and/or metadata for researchers and the general public.

CONCLUSION

In developing its collections management system and online portal, the Peabody has invested much effort in addressing the complex and variable factors raised by the introduction of online access systems; these extend well beyond cultural sensitivities to include intellectual property rights, donor agreements, and the accession status of particular records and objects. In digitizing its collections, the museum has worked hard to strike an appropriate balance between the desire for open access and the need to account for sensitive cultural factors such as nudity, the display of human remains and gravesites, sacred or ceremonial practices, and the geographical location of archaeological sites.

As the Peabody Museum continues to digitize its archival photograph collection, a substantial amount of processing will clearly be needed to create descriptive metadata at the item level and to review items for access through the Collections Online portal. Beyond the photograph collection, the archives includes a large volume of manuscripts and personal records slated for digitizing as resources become available. In the long run, digital projects in the archives have the potential to reshape academic disciplines as previously obscure records become more accessible to researchers, offering new insights into the museum's history as a collecting institution and the larger processes whereby Harvard and other research institutions have gone about constructing and preserving human culture. In a sense, digitization has promised to reopen the process of discovery that led scholars to build the Peabody collections in the first place, and with further advances in online access systems, we can expect users to find new ways to experience the museum.

NOTES

1. My thanks to Jonah Santiago and Eliana Fenyes for conducting initial interviews with Peabody staff, which laid the groundwork for my own interviews and data gathering in July 2018.

2. "About the Peabody Museum," Peabody Museum of Archeology & Ethnology, accessed August 14, 2018, https://www.peabody.harvard.edu/about.

3. "Peabody Museum Collections," Peabody Museum of Archeology & Ethnology, accessed August 14, 2018, https://www.peabody.harvard.edu/collections.

4. Page 256 of the *Official Register of Harvard University* 14, no. 12 (March 26, 1917). Reports of the President and the Treasurer of Harvard College, 1915–16, Harvard Library, accessed August 12, 2018, https://iiif.lib.harvard.edu/manifests/view/drs:427018522$1i.

Conclusion

The fourteen organizations represented in this book—which include a 206-year-old independent research library; a world-renowned museum of art and design; a network of institutions in Maine; a nonprofit, all-volunteer archive that documents the LGBT community in Boston; a national library; a collaborative of American public broadcasting stations and the Library of Congress; a university library system that has had digital initiatives for a long time; a modern art museum; a regional heritage organization with over thirty historic properties; and one of the earliest American public libraries—are striving to make their collections as accessible as possible. They have pursued this goal in a variety of ways. For example, some have simply digitized their collections, while others have also enhanced their collection management systems. Some have used social networking. Still others have incorporated digital asset management systems to organize and retrieve media, as well as to manage digital rights and permissions. A few have collaborated within their institutions, and others have found external partners. For the most part, the institutions and organizations profiled in this book have succeeded, often through strategic partnerships, innovation, and strategic planning and leadership. However, this book also gives examples of institutions that have undergone transitions: one of the museums closed down, and another one closed its library. Still another marginalized its library by moving it out of town and reducing its staffing and hours of service.

What lessons have we learned from these fourteen institutions and the more than fifty people interviewed?

SOURCES OF EVIDENCE

We drew on the following sources[1] in creating the case studies:

Documentation (emails and notes; administrative and public-use records, such as IRS 990 filings for nonprofits)
Archival records (organizational documentation, such as meeting minutes)
Interviews (with people inside the institutions as well as with others familiar with the institutions through professional or volunteer relationships)
Direct observations (based on independent visits to some of the institutions)
Physical artifacts (annual reports, publicity, and websites)
Publications (journal and newspaper articles; websites of granting agencies)

These sources gave us an understanding of how each institution or organization operates. In the case of the American Textile History Museum, which as we write (summer 2018) is in the final stages of closing down, we drew on a wider variety of sources than for any other institution.[2] The controversial decision for the Peabody Essex Museum to move its library and archives several towns away led us to the popular press, which has chronicled local reactions to the move. For "Jackman," the anonymous museum, we interviewed staff who are no longer there and read the press coverage of the museum's transition. For the other eleven institutions, we drew on the types of sources enumerated above. Several general themes emerged.

Successful Institutions Have Clear Missions

Some of these institutions post their mission statements on their websites. Here are two:

Historic New England: "We save and share New England's past to engage and inform present and future generations. Historic New England is the oldest and largest regional heritage organization in the nation. We engage diverse audiences in developing a deeper understanding and enjoyment of New England home life by being the national leader in collecting, preserving, and using significant buildings, landscapes, archives, stories, and objects from the past to today."[3]

The History Project: "Our Mission: To document and preserve the history of Boston's LGBT community, and to share that information with the public."[4]

Success Can Be Achieved with Small Budgets

Some institutions have a long history of finding ways to fund innovative initiatives. For example, long before digitization, the American Antiquarian Society (AAS), an independent research library, had a large-scale microfilming partnership with the Readex Corporation to film its preeminent newspaper collections. Later AAS digitized its newspapers. In other words, AAS has continued to build on early initiatives to make its collections as accessible as possible as it has found the resources.

Visionary Leadership and a Spirit of Collaboration Are Key Factors in Success

Since its founding in 1910 as the Society for the Preservation of New England Antiquities, Historic New England has carried on successful strategic planning.

Great Ideas

Many examples emerge from these case studies, at large institutions as well as small organizations. The National Library of Australia created PANDORA, Australia's web archive, in 1996. PANDORA is now a partnership of Australian libraries and other cultural collecting agencies. Cornell University Library was another early digital preservation innovator. More recently, the Maine Historical Society created a shared portal with dozens of LAMs in Maine.

Collaboration exists in all shapes and sizes. The American Archive of Public Broadcasting is a collaboration between the WGBH Educational Foundation, the Library of Congress, and the Corporation for Public Broadcasting. It offers a good contrast with the Maine Memory Network, with its many small institutions.

Successful Institutions Constantly Seek Ways to Improve

The Victoria and Albert Museum has found ways to support a collection management system for its enormous collections.

* * *

We divided the cases in this book into five sections based on unifying themes. The fifth, "Culturally Sensitive Materials," is represented by only one institution. We hope that more case studies will be developed in this area in the future. Increasingly, all kinds of sensitive documents and records are being discovered in libraries and archives when digitization projects are undertaken. Unfortunately, sometimes such items only "come to light" as they are being scanned. The cases can be summarized as follows.

DIGITAL STRATEGIES

The American Antiquarian Society is an independent research library with two centuries' worth of experience in collecting material and print culture up to the 1870s. While its collecting policy has a resolute focus on the past, the library has been a pioneer in using technology to expand access to its collections, beginning with microfilm in the 1950s and recently through an array of digital projects. The library's recent efforts to build up its digital capacity offer a valuable look at an institution that has proven resourceful at leveraging its technology resources to maximum benefit.

The History Project is a nonprofit archive that has long been active in documenting the LGBT community in Boston. It is a small, all-volunteer organization that offers useful lessons for local, community-based archives as they pursue growth and sustainability and contemplate steps toward digital access to paper-based collections.

Historic New England (HNE) is one of the largest and oldest regional heritage organizations in the country, and its digitization activities are well integrated with its mission and strategic planning process. It manages over thirty historic properties, an important collection of objects, artifacts, and works of art, an off-site storage facility, and a publishing program. Originally called the Society for the Preservation of New England Antiquities, it rebranded as HNE about a decade ago.

Maine Memory Network is a pioneering collaborative effort, led by the Maine Historical Society, to build a shared portal at the state level, one that has enabled dozens of libraries, archives, and museums (LAMs) in Maine to reach wider audiences than before. The experience of the Maine Memory Network shows how smaller institutions can effectively leverage their available technology resources and become genuine innovators in building online resources.

COLLABORATION WITHIN AND ACROSS INSTITUTIONS

The **American Archive of Public Broadcasting** represents a collaborative effort to preserve digital media content, an important facet of contemporary culture that falls outside traditional LAM collection boundaries, especially as it is owned by many independent broadcasters and has not been collected systematically by regional or national repositories. At the same time, the diversity of media types created by public broadcasters since the 1960s raises complex preservation issues, making it essential for the partner institutions to share their knowledge and resources. As digital media continues to evolve, this type of collaboration is likely to be a critical factor for

LAMs and other cultural organizations as they pursue their mission to collect and preserve digital culture.

The **Cornell University Library Division of Rare and Manuscript Collections'** long-term success in acquiring special collections has led to significant challenges for digital access and preservation, especially as the collections have come to include a number of new media types as well as born-digital records. In recent years, the special collections staff have responded by collaborating actively with donors and other units in the library, effectively blending curatorial expertise with the technology skills needed to capture, store, and preserve digital objects.

The library and archival collections of the **Museum of Modern Art** (MoMA) represent a vital source of documentation not just for the permanent collection but also for the history of twentieth-century art. As units in MoMA, the library and archives have managed to thrive in the face of considerable uncertainty by embracing collaboration and thoughtful strategic planning.

The **Boston Public Library**, one of the oldest public libraries in the United States, is also a major research library, with over twenty million objects in its collections. In working to expand online access to these resources, the library has taken a distinctly collaborative approach, emphasizing statewide as well as national partnerships in carrying out digitization projects and in building access systems.

STRATEGIC USE OF RESOURCES

The **Victoria and Albert Museum**, which describes itself as "the world's leading museum of art and design," has a permanent collection of over 2.3 million objects that "span 5,000 years of human creativity."[5] The vast and varied nature of the collections requires a collection management system that incorporates a variety of local curatorial practices to improve access to its holdings.

The **National Library of Australia** was early to embrace the "digital age," and it continues to do so in its projects to represent Australia's culture and history using web resources. The library has a long-standing commitment to innovation, which has fostered a culture of deep collaboration and a willingness among staff to develop new skills and to change existing practices as user expectations have continued to evolve.

INSTITUTIONS IN TRANSITION

The **Jackman Museum**, an anonymized institution, decided to close its library and lay off all its staff except for a junior archivist. The decision came as a surprise at the museum because the librarians had a stellar record of getting grants for library-museum projects. Their work was strongly supported by the previous museum director. However, the new director, two donors, and the board of trustees had their own vision for the museum—which did not include a library. This was not the first museum to close its library, and the case teaches us that libraries, museums, and archives must be in alignment if collaborations are to be successful.

The **American Textile History Museum (ATHM)**, small and private, was founded by a textile manufacturing heiress who had a sizable collection of spinning wheels, looms, and related equipment and tools. Over several decades, the museum amassed sizeable textile-related collections and a large library and archive. However, ongoing sustainability had been a challenge for quite some time—despite imaginative programming and an affiliation with the Smithsonian Institution. Several years ago, the board of trustees made the decision to close the museum. While understanding the reasons for closure is useful, this case also illustrates how an institution can best disperse its collections when transferring them becomes necessary. ATHM's process was thoughtful, and today over one hundred institutions are the lucky beneficiaries of portions of the collections, including one of the institutions included in this book: Cornell.

The **Peabody Essex Museum (PEM)** in Salem, Massachusetts, inspired a case study exploring what happens when the interests of a museum library are seen to diverge from those of the museum that it is part of. In this case, the museum used a library director's retirement as an opportunity to downsize the library staff and move the collection several towns away—despite the fact that some of those collections are directly tied to Salem. Two things make this case stand out: the museum director's twenty-year effort to downscale and diminish the library and the local community's efforts to keep the library in Salem. (Unlike most museum libraries, this collection dates back hundreds of years and originated with the museum's founders.) This case offers a striking contrast to the Museum of Modern Art in New York City, where the interests of the library, archives, and museum are well aligned.

CULTURALLY SENSITIVE MATERIALS

The **Harvard Peabody Museum of Archaeology and Ethnology** is the setting for the final case study in this book. This museum has a robust archives management program, which has been particularly active in digitizing its large photograph collection. These efforts have made available a large body of culturally sensitive information that presents both great potential value for researchers and complex ethical issues for online access.

* * *

These, then, are the institutions and organizations that have been profiled. We hope that you, too, will be able to draw lessons from them.

NOTES

1. See Robert K. Yin, "Collecting Case Study Evidence: The Principles You Should Follow in Working with Six Sources of Information," in *Case Study Research and Applications: Design and Methods*, 6th ed. (Thousand Oaks, CA: Sage, 2018), 111–38. Yin recommends these six sources. We drew on sources appropriate for each case.
2. We remain extremely grateful to staff at the American Textile History Museum for their generosity.
3. "Mission and Leadership," Historic New England, accessed September 29, 2018, https://www.historicnewengland.org/about-us/mission-leadership.
4. The History Project, accessed September 29, 2018, https://www.historyproject.org.
5. See "About Us," V&A, accessed July 16, 2018, https://www.vam.ac.uk/info/about-us.

Appendix A

Interview Questions

These questions were a starting point for our discussions and numerous wide-ranging conversations.

I. QUESTIONS FOR HIGH-LEVEL ADMINISTRATORS

Personal information:

a. Name/title
b. Academic and professional background
c. Number of years in current position
d. Number of years at current institution

1. How does digital content relate to your institution's overall mission and vision?
2. How would you describe your institution's current strategy for creating and managing digital assets, including collections and metadata?
3. How has your institution developed its online presence in recent years, including the institutional website, social media use, and digital exhibitions?
4. How do you expect your institution's digital collections and online presence to evolve over the next five to ten years?
5. How does your institution currently manage information technology, including content or collection management systems (i.e., in a centralized or decentralized manner)? (In other words, is it done in more than one place?)

6. Has the rise of digital media and collections led to more or less collaboration across departments or functional areas within the institution and with other institutions?
7. Can you identify particular institutional challenges in digital collections management, including organizational factors and resource constraints?
8. Can you point to experimental or innovative digital projects within your institution over the past five to ten years? If so, what influence have these projects had on the organization as a whole?
9. Which funding sources have been most important in supporting digital projects or initiatives, particularly grants versus internal resources?
10. How would you describe your institution's current priorities for digitization and online access? Which collections does the institution view as most in demand or most valuable?

II. QUESTIONS FOR IT STAFF

Personal information:

a. Name/title
b. Academic and professional background
c. Number of years in current position
d. Number of years at current institution

1. What major systems does your institution currently use for managing digital collections, including content management systems, integrated library systems, museum collection management systems, and so forth?
2. How does your organization support workflows leading to the creation of new digital assets, including digitization services and metadata creation?
3. How does your organization support access to existing digital assets, including online exhibitions, digital humanities projects, online catalogs or finding aids, and institutional repositories for public access?
4. Does your institution currently have formal digital preservation plans? If so, how are the plans being implemented?
5. How does your institution currently manage information technology (i.e., in a centralized or decentralized manner)? Does it use formal or informal reporting structures? How much collaboration across departmental structures is involved in managing IT infrastructure and services?

6. How would you describe your institution's relationship with IT vendors, both now and in the past? How are contracts with outside vendors managed? Has your institution recently changed vendors? Are you considering changing vendors in the near future?
7. How does your institution currently test and evaluate existing systems, services, and digital workflows?
8. Can you point to innovative IT projects or new systems or services that have had a significant impact on the institution as a whole?
9. What challenges and opportunities do you currently see for your institution involving IT at present?
10. How do you envision technology evolving over the next five to ten years, both for your institution and more generally for the LAM sector?

III. QUESTIONS FOR CURATORS AND COLLECTION MANAGERS

Personal information:

a. Name/title
b. Academic and professional background
c. Number of years in current position
d. Number of years at current institution

1. Please describe your current role in managing digital as well as material collections.
2. What types and quantities of digital assets are currently managed by your department?
3. To what extent have you and your department been involved in digitization efforts or in creating digital assets over the past five to ten years?
4. How does your organization manage workflows for creating and managing digital assets? Do you have formal, routine procedures for ingesting digital content into repository or content management systems? Do you have written manuals for creating and transferring digital assets?
5. Which metadata standards or schemas does your institution currently use in describing collection objects?
6. How are digital assets stored at present? Please describe the key technologies used by your organization for digital collections.
7. Does your institution currently have formal digital preservation plans? If so, how are the plans being implemented?

8. How does your organization support access to digital assets, including online exhibitions and institutional repositories for public access? How do you expect your institution's online presence to evolve over the next five to ten years?
9. Have digital media and collections led to more or less collaboration across departments or functional areas within the institution? Have digital projects and collections led to collaborations with other LAM institutions?
10. Can you identify particular institutional challenges in digital collections management, including organizational factors and resource constraints?
11. Can you point to experimental or innovative digital projects within your department over the past five to ten years? If so, what impact have these projects had on the department and the institution as a whole? Are you currently planning new digital projects that you expect will lead to changes in how your department creates or manages digital assets?

Developed with the support of the Emily Hollowell Research Fund (2015–2016) project titled "Learning from the LAMs: Case Studies and Teaching Scenarios on Digital Collections Management."

Appendix B

Interviewees

Note that some interviewees chose not to be identified.

- Allegretto, Kim (Harvard Peabody Museum)
- Amoroso, Kathy (Maine Historical Society/The Maine Memory Network)
- Barbash, Barbara (Harvard Peabody Museum)
- Blake, Tom (Boston Public Library)
- Bouvier, Libby (The History Project)
- Bradley, Kevin (National Library of Australia)
- Cariani, Karen (American Archive of Public Broadcasting)
- Carter, Kevin (American Archive of Public Broadcasting)
- Coleman, Jim (American Textile History Museum)
- Condon, Lorna (Historic New England)
- Conti, Nick (American Antiquarian Society)
- Cricks, Marion (Victoria & Albert Museum)
- Curtis, Rachel (Library of Congress/American Archive of Public Broadcasting)
- Davis, Casey (American Archive of Public Broadcasting)
- DeBono, David (Harvard Peabody Museum of Archaeology and Ethnology)
- Dietrich, Dianne (Cornell University Library)
- Dunlap, Ellen (American Antiquarian Society)
- Dwiggins, David (Historic New England)
- Elder, Andrew (The History Project)
- Elligott, Michelle (Museum of Modern Art)

Faulder, Erin (Cornell University Library)
Fraimow, Rebecca (American Archive of Public Broadcasting)
Gevinson, Alan (Library of Congress/American Archive of Public Broadcasting)
Hardy, Molly O'Hagan (American Antiquarian Society)
Hewes, Lauren (American Antiquarian Society)
Hirbour, Kathy (American Textile History Museum)
Holden, William (The History Project)
Hopper, Kayla Haveles (American Antiquarian Society)
Hughston, Milan (Museum of Modern Art)
Kervick, Patricia (Harvard Peabody Museum of Archaeology and Ethnology)
Kiorgaard, Deirdre (National Library of Australia)
Knoles, Thomas (American Antiquarian Society)
Laskey, Tilly (Maine Historical Society/The Maine Memory Network)
Leonard, David (Boston Public Library)
Mackenzie, Amelia (National Library of Australia)
McCallum, Chuck (American Archive for Public Broadcasting)
Meyers, Drew (American Archive for Public Broadcasting)
Montgomery, Rita (Harvard Peabody Museum of Archaeology and Ethnology)
Platzer, Cornel (National Library of Australia)
Pucci, Danielle (Boston Public Library)
Roosa, Sadie (American Archive of Public Broadcasting)
Rothman, Steve (Harvard Peabody Museum of Archaeology and Ethnology)
Sauer, Anne (Cornell University Library)
Sheridan, Claire (American Textile History Museum)
Smith, Allison (American Archive of Public Broadcasting)
Vasta, Meredith (Harvard Peabody Museum of Archaeology and Ethnology)
Ward, Jane (American Textile History Museum)
Wong, David (National Library of Australia)
Wong, Wan (National Library of Australia)
Young-Gomes, Cindi (Maine Historical Society/The Maine Memory Network)

Bibliography

Adams, Nancy E., Maureen A. Gaffney, and Valerie Lynn. 2016. "The Role of Evidence-Based Practice in Collaborations between Academic Librarians and Education Faculty." *portal: Libraries and the Academy* 16, no. 4: 697–720. doi:10.1353/pla.2016.0048.

Adu, Kofi Koranteng, and Patrick Ngulube. 2016. "Preserving the Digital Heritage of Public Institutions in Ghana in the Wake of Electronic Government." *Library Hi Tech* 34, no. 4 (November 21): 748–63. doi:10.1108/lht-07-2016-0077.

Alberti, Samuel J. M. M., Stephen Allen, Xavier Dectot, and Ruth Gill. 2018. "Reflecting the Now: Project Management and Contemporary Collecting in a Multi-disciplinary Museum." *Museum and Society* 15, no. 3 (January): 324–42. https://journals.le.ac.uk/ojs1/index.php/mas/article/view/2427 (accessed May 17, 2018).

Allard, Suzie. 2002. "Digital Libraries and Organizations for International Collaboration and Knowledge Creation." *Electronic Library* 20, no. 5 (October): 369–81. doi:10.1108/02640470210447793.

Arns, Jennifer Weil, ed. 2016. *Annual Review of Cultural Heritage Informatics*. Lanham, MD: Rowman & Littlefield.

Art Libraries Society of North America (ARLIS). 2016. "State of Art Museum Libraries 2016." ARLIS/NA Museum Division White Paper. ARLIS. https://www.arlisna.org/images/researchreports/State_of_Art_Museum_Libraries_2016.pdf (accessed August 13, 2019).

Battley, Belinda. 2017. "Co-producing Archival Research with Communication, Reflexivity and Friendship: Crossing the Three-Wire Bridge." *Archival Science* 17, no. 4 (August 18): 371–91. doi:10.1007/s10502-017-9279-y.

Bernier, Hélène, and Mathieu Viau-Courville. 2017. "Curating Action: Rethinking Ethnographic Collections and the Role/Place of Performing Arts in the Museum." *Museum and Society* 14, no. 2 (June): 237–52. https://journals.le.ac.uk/ojs1/index.php/mas/article/view/641 (accessed May 17, 2018).

Biedermann, Bernadette. 2017. "'Virtual Museums' as Digital Collection Complexes. A Museological Perspective Using the Example of Hans-Gross-Kriminalmuseum." *Museum Management and Curatorship* 32, no. 3 (May 7): 281–97. doi:10.1080/09647775.2017.1322916.

Borgman, Christine. 1999. "What Are Digital Libraries? Competing Visions." *Information Processing and Management* 35, no. 3 (May): 227–43.

Bryant, Julius. 2017. *Designing the V&A: The Museum as a Work of Art*. London: Lund Humphries.

Burroughs, Jennie M. 2017. "No Uniform Culture: Patterns of Collaborative Research in the Humanities." *portal: Libraries and the Academy* 17, no. 3: 507–27. doi:10.1353/pla.2017.0032.

Cannon, San. 2015. "Content Curation for Research: A Framework for Building a 'Data Museum.'" *International Journal of Digital Curation* 10, no. 2 (July 28): 58–68. doi:10.2218/ijdc.v10i2.355.

Cariani, Karen, and Casey Davis. 2014. "Challenges, Workflows and Insights in the Collaboration to Preserve America's Public Media." Paper delivered at the New England Archivists Meeting, Newport, Rhode Island, fall.

Chen, Chih-Ming, and Ming-Yueh Tsay. 2017. "Applications of Collaborative Annotation System in Digital Curation, Crowdsourcing, and Digital Humanities." *Electronic Library* 35, no. 6 (November 6): 1122–40. doi:10.1108/el-08-2016-0172.

Cocciolo, Anthony. 2016. "When Archivists and Digital Asset Managers Collide: Tensions and Ways Forward." *American Archivist* 79, no. 1 (spring/summer): 121–36.

Colwell, Chip. 2017. *Plundered Skulls and Stolen Spirits: Inside the Fight to Reclaim Native America's Culture*. Chicago: University of Chicago Press.

Conrad, Suzanna K. 2012. "Analog, the Sequel: An Analysis of Current Film Archiving Practice and Hesitance to Embrace Digital Preservation." *Archival Issues* 34, no. 1: 27–43.

Corrall, Sheila. 2014. "Designing Libraries for Research Collaboration in the Network World: An Exploratory Study." *LIBER Quarterly* 24, no. 1 (August 4): 17. doi:10.18352/lq.9525.

Daniels, Caroline, Heather Fox, Sarah-Jane Poindexter, and Elizabeth Reilly. 2015. "Saving All the Freaks on the Life Raft: Blending Documentation Strategy with Community Engagement to Build a Local Music Archives." *American Archivist* 78, no. 1 (spring/summer): 238–61.

Delaney, Beth, and Annemieke de Jong. 2015. "Media Archives and Digital Preservation: Overcoming Cultural Barriers." *New Review of Information Networking* 20, no. 1–2: 73–89. doi:10.1080/13614576.2015.1112626.

Denzin, Norman K., and Yvonna S. Lincoln. 2005. *The Sage Handbook of Qualitative Research*. 3rd ed. Thousand Oaks, CA: Sage.

———. 2011. *The Sage Handbook of Qualitative Research*. 4th ed. Thousand Oaks, CA: Sage.

Deridder, Jody L., and Alissa Matheny Helms. 2016. "Intake of Digital Content: Survey Results from the Field." *D-Lib Magazine* 22, no. 11/12 (November). doi:10.1045/november2016-deridder.

Dilevko, Juris, and Lisa Gottlieb. 2004. *The Evolution of Library and Museum Partnerships: Historical Antecedents, Contemporary Manifestations, and Future Directions*. Westport, CT: Libraries Unlimited.

Drachen, Thea Marie, Ole Ellegaard, Asger Væring Larsen, and Søren Bertil Fabricius Dorch. 2016. "Sharing Data Increases Citations." *LIBER Quarterly* 26, no. 2 (August): 67–82. doi:10.18352/lq.10149.

Ewin, Timothy A. M., and Joanne V. Ewin. 2015. "In Defence of the Curator: Maximising Museum Impact." *Museum Management and Curatorship* 31, no. 4 (September 15): 322–30. doi:10.1080/09647775.2015.1060865.

Exell, Karen. 2017. "Desiring the Past and Reimagining the Present: Contemporary Collecting in Qatar." *Museum and Society* 14, no. 2 (June): 259–74. https://journals.le.ac.uk/ojs1/index.php/mas/article/view/642 (accessed May 17, 2018).

Eyre, Jodi Reeves, John C. Maclachlan, and Christa Williford, eds. 2017. *A Splendid Torch: Learning and Teaching in Today's Academic Libraries*. Washington, DC: Council on Library and Information Resources. September. https://www.clir.org/pubs/reports/pub174 (accessed September 26, 2018).

Feng, Yuanyuan, and Lorraine Richards. 2018. "A Review of Digital Curation Professional Competencies: Theory and Current Practices." *Records Management Journal* 28, no. 1 (March 19): 62–78. doi:10.1108/rmj-09-2016-0022.

Gabriel, Mille. 2017. "New Futures for Old Collections—Contemporary Collecting and Community Involvement at the National Museum of Denmark." *Museum and Society* 14, no. 2 (June): 275–93. https://journals.le.ac.uk/ojs1/index.php/mas/article/view/643 (accessed May 17, 2018).

Gilman, Neyda V., Jimena Sagàs, Matt Camper, and Andrew P. Norton. 2017. "A Faculty-Librarian Collaboration Success Story: Implementing a Teach-the-Teacher Library and Information Literacy Instruction Model in a First-Year Agricultural Science Course." *Library Trends* 65, no. 3: 339–58. doi:10.1353/lib.2017.0005.

Godfrey, Bruce, and Jeremy Kenyon. 2017. "The USDA's NAIP Imagery in Idaho: A Decade of Evolving Partnerships to Improve Access." *Library Trends* 65, no. 3: 414–28. doi:10.1353/lib.2017.0009.

Greffe, Xavier, Anne Krebs, and Sylvie Pflieger. 2017. "The Future of the Museum in the Twenty-First Century: Recent Clues from France." *Museum Management and Curatorship* 32, no. 4 (April 19): 319–34. doi:10.1080/09647775.2017.1313126.

Greider, Antoinette Paris, and Barbara S. Hutchinson. 2017. "The United States Agricultural Information Network: Accomplishments through Strategic Collaboration." *Library Trends* 65, no. 3: 253–78. doi:10.1353/lib.2017.0001.

Handel, Dinah. 2018. "Data Migration, Digital Asset Management and Microservices at CUNY TV." *The Signal: Digital Preservation* (blog). March 14. https://blogs.loc.gov/thesignal/2016/03/data-migration-digital-asset-management-and-microservices-at-cuny-tv (accessed May 17, 2018).

Hastings, Samantha K., ed. 2014. *Annual Review of Cultural Heritage Informatics*. Lanham, MD: Rowman & Littlefield.

Hays, Anne. 2018. "Zine Authors' Attitudes about Inclusion in Public and Academic Library Collections: A Survey-Based Study." *Library Quarterly* 88, no. 1 (January): 60–78. doi:10.1086/694869.

Hirayama, Hina. 2013. *"With Eclat": The Boston Athenaeum and the Origin of the Museum of Fine Arts, Boston.* Boston: Boston Athenaeum.

Hogenboom, Karen, and Michele Hayslett. 2017. "Pioneers in the Wild West: Managing Data Collections." *portal: Libraries and the Academy* 17, no. 2: 295–319. doi:10.1353/pla.2017.0018.

Hoogwaerts, Leanne. 2017. "Museums, Exchanges, and Their Contribution to Joseph Nye's Concept of 'Soft Power.'" *Museum and Society* 14, no. 2 (June): 313–22. https://journals.le.ac.uk/ojs1/index.php/mas/article/view/645 (accessed May 17, 2018).

Horn, Christine. 2018. "Making Sense: Experiential Engagements with Ethnographic Photographs." *Museum and Society* 15, no. 3 (January): 301–23. https://journals.le.ac.uk/ojs1/index.php/mas/article/view/2542 (accessed May 17, 2018).

Houghton, Bernadette. 2016. "Preservation Challenges in the Digital Age." *D-Lib Magazine* 22, no. 7/8 (July). doi:10.1045/july2016-houghton.

Hudson, Claire. 2012. "The Digital Museum." In *Evaluating and Measuring the Value, Use and Impact of Digital Collections*, edited by Lorna M. Hughes, 35–48. London: Facet Publishing.

Hughes, Lorna, ed. 2012. *Evaluating and Measuring the Value, Use and Impact of Digital Collections.* London: Facet Publishing.

Hutchison, Fiona C., Adrian R. Bailey, and Tim E. Coles. 2018. "An Evidence Based Methodology for Cultural Institutions Seeking to Identify and Profile Their Local Populations." *Museum Management and Curatorship* 33, no. 1 (January 2): 96–114. doi:10.1080/09647775.2017.1420484.

Joffrion, Elizabeth, and Natalia Fernández. 2015. "Collaborations between Tribal and Nontribal Organizations: Suggested Best Practices for Sharing Expertise, Cultural Resources, and Knowledge." *American Archivist* 78, no. 1 (spring/summer): 192–237.

Kalfatovic, Martin R., Effie Kapsalis, Katherine P. Spiess, Anne Van Camp, and Michael Edson. 2008. "Smithsonian Team Flickr: A Library, Archives, and Museums Collaboration in Web 2.0 Space." *Archival Science* 8, no. 4 (December): 267–77.

Keith, Brian W., Bonnie J. Smith, and Laurie N. Taylor. 2017. "Building a Collaborative Position Description Archive as a Community of Practice." *portal: Libraries and the Academy* 17, no. 2: 419–34. doi:10.1353/pla.2017.0026.

Kidd, Jenny, and Rosie Cardiff. 2017. "'A Space of Negotiation': Visitor Generated Content and Ethics at Tate." *Museum and Society* 15, no. 1 (June): 43–55. https://journals.le.ac.uk/ojs1/index.php/mas/article/view/661 (accessed May 17, 2018).

Kim, Jeonghyun, Edward Warga, and William Moen. 2013. "Competencies Required for Digital Curation: An Analysis of Job Advertisements." *International Journal of Digital Curation* 8, no. 1 (June 14): 66–83. doi:10.2218/ijdc.v8i1.242.

Kirkwood, Rachel Joy. 2016. "Collection Development or Data-Driven Content Curation? An Exploratory Project in Manchester." *Library Management* 37, no. 4/5 (June 13): 275–84. doi:10.1108/lm-05-2016-0044.

Kling, Rob. 1999. "What Is Social Informatics and Why Does It Matter?" *D-Lib Magazine* 5, no. 1 (January). http://www.dlib.org/dlib/january99/kling/01kling.html (accessed May 17, 2018).

Koloniari, Maria, and Kostas Fassoulis. 2017. "Knowledge Management Perceptions in Academic Libraries." *Journal of Academic Librarianship* 43, no. 2 (March): 135–42. doi:10.1016/j.acalib.2016.11.006.

Kruse, Filip, and Jesper Boserup Thestrup. 2014. "Research Libraries' New Role in Research Data Management, Current Trends and Visions in Denmark." *LIBER Quarterly* 23, no. 4 (April 15): 310. doi:10.18352/lq.9173.

Laursen, Ditte, Christian Hviid Mortensen, Anne Rørbæk Olesen, and Kim Christian Schrøder. 2017. "'I ♥ Skagens Museum': Patterns of Interaction in the Institutional Facebook Communication of Museums." *Museum and Society* 15, no. 2: 171–92. https://journals.le.ac.uk/ojs1/index.php/mas/article/view/831 (accessed May 17, 2018).

Luísa Cabral, Maria. 1992. "Collaboration in the Creation of National Bibliographic Resources." *Electronic Library* 10, no. 2 (February): 93–95. doi:10.1108/eb045128.

Lynch, Clifford. 1999. "Institutional Repositories: Essential Infrastructure for Scholarship in the Digital Age." *portal: Libraries and the Academy* 3, no. 2 (January): 327–36.

———. 2017. "Stewardship in the 'Age of Algorithms.'" *First Monday* 22, no. 12 (December 2). doi:10.5210/fm.v22i12.8097.

Manžuch, Zinaida. 2011. "Collaborative Networks of Memory Institutions in Digitisation Initiatives." *Electronic Library* 29, no. 3 (June 7): 320–43. doi:10.1108/02640471111141070.

Maron, Nancy L., Sarah Pickle, and Deanna Marcum. 2013. *Searching for Sustainability: Strategies from Eight Digitized Special Collections*. Ithaka S+R. http://sr.ithaka.org/wp-content/uploads/2015/08/SR_IMLS_20140129.pdf (accessed May 17, 2018).

Marsh, Diana E., Ricardo L. Punzalan, Robert Leopold, Brian Butler, and Massimo Petrozzi. 2015. "Stories of Impact: The Role of Narrative in Understanding the Value and Impact of Digital Collections." *Archival Science* 16, no. 4 (September 4): 327–72. doi:10.1007/s10502-015-9253-5.

Marty, Paul F. 2006. "Finding the Skills for Tomorrow: Information Literacy and Museum Information Professionals." *Museum Management and Curatorship* 21, no. 4: 317–35.

———. 2007a. "The Changing Nature of Information Work in Museums." *Journal of the American Society for Information Science and Technology* 58, no. 1: 97–107.

———. 2007b. "Museum Professionals and the Relevance of LIS Expertise." *Library & Information Science Research* 29, no. 2: 252–76.

Marty, Paul F., and Katherine Burton Jones, eds. 2008. *Museum Informatics: People, Information, and Technology in Museums*. New York: Routledge.

Marty, Paul F., and Michael B. Twidale. 2011. "Museum Informatics across the Curriculum: Ten Years of Preparing LIS Students for Careers Transcending Libraries, Archives, and Museums." *Journal of Education for Library and Information Science* 52, no. 1: 9–16.

Mason, Marco. 2015. "Prototyping Practices Supporting Interdisciplinary Collaboration in Digital Media Design for Museums." *Museum Management and Curatorship* 30, no. 5 (October): 394–426. doi:10.1080/09647775.2015.1086667.

Mattock, Lindsay Kistler, Colleen Theisen, and Jennifer Burek Pierce. 2017. "A Case for Digital Squirrels: Using and Preserving YouTube for Popular Culture Research." *First Monday* 23, no. 1 (December 31). doi:10.5210/fm.v23i1.8163.

McCollough, Aaron. 2017. "Does It Make a Sound: Are Open Access Monographs Discoverable in Library Catalogs?" *portal: Libraries and the Academy* 17, no. 1: 179–94. doi:10.1353/pla.2017.0010.

McKnight, David, and Eric Pumroy. 2015. "The Challenges of Sustaining a Long-Term Collaboration: Reflections on the Philadelphia Hidden Collections Projects." *Innovation, Col-*

laboration, and Models: Proceedings of the CLIR Cataloging Hidden Special Collections and Archives Symposium, March 2015. Council on Library and Information Resources. http://www.clir.org/wp-content/uploads/sites/6/mcknightetal.pdf (accessed September 26, 2018).

McRostie, Donna. 2016. "The Only Constant Is Change." *Library Management* 37, no. 6/7 (August 8): 363–72. doi:10.1108/lm-04-2016-0027.

Meier, John J. 2016. "The Future of Academic Libraries: Conversations with Today's Leaders about Tomorrow." *portal: Libraries and the Academy* 16, no. 2 (April): 263–88. http://muse.jhu.edu/article/613842 (accessed May 17, 2018).

Mudogo Mutula, Stephen. 2014. "Status of Digital Heritage Preservation Management in Eastern Africa." *Electronic Library* 32, no. 3 (May 27): 363–74. doi:10.1108/el-01-2013-0003.

National Film Preservation Board. 1997. *Television and Video Preservation: A Report on the Current State of American Television and Video Preservation*. Washington, DC: Library of Congress.

Neatrour, Anna, Matt Brunsvik, Sean Buckner, Brian McBride, and Jeremy Myntti. 2014. "The SIMP Tool: Facilitating Digital Library, Metadata, and Preservation Workflow at the University of Utah's J. Willard Marriott Library." *D-Lib Magazine* 20, no. 7/8 (July). doi:10.1045/july2014-neatrour.

Niu, Jinfang. 2014. "Appraisal and Selection for Digital Curation." *International Journal of Digital Curation* 9, no. 2 (October 23): 65–82. doi:10.2218/ijdc.v9i2.272.

OCLC Coalition to Advance Learning in Archives, Libraries and Museums. 2017. "Collective Wisdom: An Exploration of Library, Archives and Museum Cultures" (White paper, OCLC Research, Dublin, Ohio).

Oestreicher, Cheryl, ed. 2015. *Innovation, Collaboration and Models: Proceedings of the CLIR Cataloging Hidden Special Collections and Archives Symposium, March 2015*. Council on Library and Information Resources. November. http://www.clir.org/pubs/reports/pub169 (accessed September 26, 2018).

Olsen, Livia, Julie Kelly, and Noël Kopriva. 2017. "The Agriculture Network Information Collaborative (AgNIC): Building on the Past, Looking to the Future." *Library Trends* 65, no. 3: 279–92. doi:10.1353/lib.2017.0002.

Papadakis, Ioannis, Konstantinos Kyprianos, and Michalis Stefanidakis. 2015. "Linked Data URIs and Libraries: The Story So Far." *D-Lib Magazine* 21, no. 5/6 (May). doi:10.1045/may2015-papadakis.

Parilla, Lesley, and Meghan Ferriter. 2016. "Social Media and Crowdsourced Transcription of Historical Materials at the Smithsonian Institution: Methods for Strengthening Community Engagement and Its Tie to Transcription Output." *American Archivist* 79, no. 2 (fall/winter): 438–60.

Pettersen, Lene. 2017. "Sorting Things Out: A Typology of the Digital Collaborative Economy." *First Monday* 22, no. 8 (July 31). doi:10.5210/fm.v22i8.7805.

Poole, Alex H. 2016. "The Conceptual Landscape of Digital Curation." *Journal of Documentation* 72, no. 5 (September 12): 961–86. doi:10.1108/jd-10-2015-0123.

Prestopnik, Nathan. 2013. "Cooperative Visualization: A Design Case." *Library Hi Tech* 31, no. 2 (June 7): 371–90. doi:10.1108/07378831311329112.

Prieto, Adolfo G. 2009. "From Conceptual to Perceptual Reality: Trust in Digital Repositories." *Library Review* 58, no. 8 (September 4): 593–606. doi:10.1108/00242530910987082.

Punzalan, Ricardo L., and Adam Kriesberg. 2017. "Library-Mediated Collaborations: Data Curation at the National Agricultural Library." *Library Trends* 65, no. 3: 429–47. doi:10.1353/lib.2017.0010.

Ratanya, Felicitas Ciabere. 2017. "Institutional Repository: Access and Use by Academic Staff at Egerton University, Kenya." *Library Management* 38, no. 4/5 (June 13): 276–84. doi:10.1108/lm-02-2017-0018.

Ray, Joyce. 2012. "The Rise of Digital Curation and Cyberinfrastructure." *Library Hi Tech* 30, no. 4 (November 16): 604–22. doi:10.1108/07378831211285086.

———. 2017. "Digital Curation in Museums." *Library Hi Tech* 35, no. 1 (March 20): 32–39. doi:10.1108/lht-12-2016-0154.

Richards, Lorraine L. 2016. "Teaching Data Creators How to Develop an OAIS-Compliant Digital Curation System: Colearning and Breakdowns in Support of Requirements Analysis." *American Archivist* 79, no. 2 (fall/winter): 371–91.

Rimkus, Kyle, Thomas Padilla, Tracy Popp, and Greer Martin. 2014. "Digital Preservation File Format Policies of ARL Member Libraries: An Analysis." *D-Lib Magazine* 20, no. 3/4 (March). doi:10.1045/march2014-rimkus.

Rius-Ulldemolins, Joaquim. 2015. "The Rise of the Hybrid Model of Art Museums and Cultural Institutions. The Case of Barcelona." *Museum Management and Curatorship* 31, no. 2 (November 12): 178–92. doi:10.1080/09647775.2015.1107853.

Robinson, Helena. 2015. "'A Lot of People Going That Extra Mile': Professional Collaboration and Cross-Disciplinarity in Converged Collecting Institutions." *Museum Management and Curatorship* 31, no. 2 (September 15): 141–58. doi:10.1080/09647775.2015.1070368.

Rolan, Gregory. 2016. "Agency in the Archive: A Model for Participatory Recordkeeping." *Archival Science* 17, no. 3 (July 5): 195–225. doi:10.1007/s10502-016-9267-7.

Ryholt, Kim. 2013. "Libraries in Ancient Egypt." In *Ancient Libraries*, edited by Jason König, Katerina Oikonomopoulou, and Greg Woolf, 23–37. Cambridge: Cambridge University Press.

Saarti, Jarmo, Markku Antero Laitinen, and Pentti Vattulainen. 2017. "Effects of the Digitization to the Printed Collection Policies." *Library Management* 38, no. 2/3 (March 14): 167–74. doi:10.1108/lm-01-2017-0004.

Schrimpf, Sabine, and Christian Keitel. 2014. "Nestor Guideline for Preservation Planning—A Process Model." *LIBER Quarterly* 23, no. 3 (February 12): 201. doi:10.18352/lq.9166.

Science and Technology Council. 2011. *Long-Term Management and Storage of Digital Motion Picture Materials: A Digital Motion Picture Archive Framework Project Case Study*. Hollywood, CA: Academy of Motion Picture Arts and Sciences.

Sheehan, Beth, and Karen Hogenboom. 2017. "Assessing a Patron-Driven, Library-Funded Data Purchase Program." *Journal of Academic Librarianship* 43, no. 1 (January): 49–56. doi:10.1016/j.acalib.2016.10.001.

Skinner, Julia. 2017. "Innovation in Harlem: Using the Change in Historic Institutions Model to Study a Public Library's Development." *Library Quarterly* 87, no. 2 (April): 136–49. doi:10.1086/690738.

Sorin, Gretchen Sullivan, and Lynne A. Sessions, eds. 2015. *Case Studies in Cultural Entrepreneurship: How to Create Relevant and Sustainable Institutions*. Lanham, MD: Rowman & Littlefield.

Stapleton, Suzanne, Christine Fruin, Christy Shorey, Laurie N. Taylor, and Chelsea Dinsmore. 2017. "Partnerships in Agricultural Publications: University of Florida's Marston Science Library and the Florida State Horticultural Society." *Library Trends* 65, no. 3: 359–77. doi:10.1353/lib.2017.0006.

Stein, Ayla, and Santi Thompson. 2015. "Taking Control: Identifying Motivations for Migrating Library Digital Asset Management Systems." *D-Lib Magazine* 21, no. 9/10 (September). doi:10.1045/september2015-stein.

Suber, Peter. 2012. *Open Access*. Cambridge, MA: MIT Press.

Tella, Adeyinka. 2016. "Knowledge-Sharing Intention among Information Professionals in Nigeria: A Statistical Analysis." *portal: Libraries and the Academy* 16, no. 2 (April): 225–23. http://muse.jhu.edu/article/613840 (accessed May 17, 2018).

Termens, Miquel, Mireia Ribera, and Anita Locher. 2015. "An Analysis of File Format Control in Institutional Repositories." *Library Hi Tech* 33, no. 2 (June 15): 162–74. doi:10.1108/lht-10-2014-0098.

Tharani, Karim. 2012. "Collections Digitization Framework: A Service-Oriented Approach to Digitization in Academic Libraries." *Partnership: The Canadian Journal of Library and Information Practice and Research* 7, no. 2: 1–13.

Way, Doug. 2017. "Transforming Monograph Collections with a Model of Collections as a Service." *portal: Libraries and the Academy* 17, no. 2: 283–94. doi:10.1353/pla.2017.0017.

Weisbrod, Dirk. 2016. "Cloud-Supported Preservation of Digital Papers: A Solution for Special Collections?" *LIBER Quarterly* 25, no. 3 (February): 136–51. doi:10.18352/lq.10114.

Wellisch, Hans H. 1994. “Alexandrian Library.” In *Encyclopedia of Library History*, edited by Wayne A. Wiegand and Donald G. Davis Jr., 19–21. New York: Garland Publishing.

Whiteley, Louise, Anette Stenslund, Ken Arnold, and Thomas Söderqvist. 2017. “‘The House’ as a Framing Device for Public Engagement in STEM Museums.” *Museum and Society* 15, no. 2: 217–35. https://journals.le.ac.uk/ojs1/index.php/mas/article/view/833 (accessed May 17, 2018).

Wilk, Christopher, and Nick Humphrey, eds. 2004. *Creating the British Galleries at the V&A*. London: V&A Publications.

Wilson, Thomas C. 2017. “Rethinking Digital Preservation: Definitions, Models, and Requirements.” *Digital Library Perspectives* 33, no. 2 (May 8): 128–36. doi:10.1108/dlp-08-2016-0029.

Wright, Richard. 2012. *Preserving Moving Picture and Sound*. DPC Technology Watch Series. York, UK: Digital Preservation Coalition. http://dx.doi.org/10.7207/twr12-01 (accessed May 17, 2018).

Yaco, Sonia, Caroline Brown, and Lee Konrad. 2016. “Linking Special Collections to Classrooms: A Curriculum-to-Collection Crosswalk.” *American Archivist* 79, no. 2 (fall/winter): 417–37.

Yin, Robert K. 2018. *Case Study Research and Applications: Design and Methods*. 6th ed. Thousand Oaks, CA: Sage.

Zinkham, Helena, and Michelle Springer. 2011. “Taking Photographs to the People: The Flickr Commons Project and the Library of Congress.” In *A Different Kind of Web: New Connections between Archives and Our Users*, edited by Kate Theimer, 102–15. Chicago: Society of American Archivists.

Zoller, Gabriela, and Katie DeMarsh. 2013. “Museum Cataloging from a Library and Information Science Perspective.” *Art Documentation* 32, no. 1 (spring): 54–70.

Zorich, Diane M., Günter Waibel, and Ricky Erway. 2008. *Beyond the Silos of the LAMs: Collaboration among Libraries, Archives and Museums*. Dublin, OH: OCLC Research. http://www.oclc.org/research/publications/library/2008/2008-05.pdf (accessed May 17, 2018).

Index

About the Authors and Contributors

AUTHORS

Peter Botticelli is assistant professor at the School of Library and Information Science at Simmons in Boston, where he teaches courses in digital stewardship, digital asset management, and archives appraisal. Botticelli has AM and PhD degrees in history from the University of Illinois at Urbana-Champaign and an MSI degree with a concentration in archives and records management from the University of Michigan. He previously taught at the University of Arizona School of Information Resources and Library Science, where he directed the school's graduate certificate program in digital information management. Botticelli has also held research positions at Cornell University Library, the University of Michigan, and Harvard Business School.

Martha R. Mahard managed the print and photograph inventory projects at the Boston Public Library (BPL). Before joining the BPL, she was professor of practice at the School of Library and Information Science at Simmons in Boston, where she taught courses in the management of photographic archives, art documentation, and preservation management. She also held a variety of positions in the Harvard University libraries, including the Harvard Theatre Collection, the Graduate School of Design's Frances Loeb Library, and the Fine Arts Library, where she was curator of historic photographs. During her thirty-five years at Harvard, she was instrumental in the development and implementation of its first online union catalog for visual materials. She holds a BA in English literature from Barnard College, an MA in theater history from Tufts University, and an MLIS and a doctor of arts in library administration from Simmons. She is coauthor of *The Preservation Management Handbook: A 21st-Century Guide for Libraries, Archives, and Museums* (2014).

Michèle V. Cloonan is professor at and former dean of the School of Library and Information Science at Simmons in Boston. Immediately prior to that, she was associate professor and chair in the Department of Information Studies at the University of California, Los Angeles. Her area of expertise is the preservation of cultural heritage, though she has published widely in other areas as well. Cloonan has an AB in literature from Bennington College, an AM in literature and art history from the University of Chicago, and MS and PhD degrees in library and information science from the University of Illinois. Her 2015 book *Preserving Our Heritage* won the Society of American Archivists award for best preservation publication. Her most recent book, *The Monumental Challenge of Preservation*, was published in 2018.

CONTRIBUTORS

Emeline Dehn-Reynolds is the traditional music and dance archivist at the University of New Hampshire's Milne Special Collections and Archives. Her research focuses on the history of New England's contra and square dance and its musical evolution, with special interest in the contribution of minority and historically marginalized populations. She graduated from Simmons with a master's degree in library and information science in 2017.

Brett Freiburger is the digitization project supervisor in the Boston Public Library's Print Department and a contract archivist for the Congregational Library and Archives, also in Boston. Since graduating from Simmons with a master's degree in library and information science, Freiburger has served as director of the Babcock Library in Ashford, Connecticut, as a manuscript assistant at Harvard University's Schlesinger Library, and as an assistant collections manager at the Harriet Beecher Stowe Center.

Ross Harvey is adjunct professor at Monash University, Melbourne, having previously held academic positions at universities in Australia, Singapore, and the United States. His research interests focus on the stewardship of digital materials in libraries and archives, particularly on their preservation. Ross has published widely in the fields of bibliographic organization, library education, the preservation of library and archival material, and newspaper history. His most recent books are (with Jaye Weatherburn) *Preserving Digital Materials*, 3rd ed. (2018) and (with Gillian Oliver) *Digital Curation*, 2nd ed. (2016).

Bryce Roe is manager of audio preservation services at the Northeast Document Conservation Center (NEDCC). Prior to joining NEDCC, she worked as a project archivist at the University of Massachusetts, Dartmouth, Archives and Special Collections. She graduated in 2016 with a master's degree in library and information science from Simmons, where she was president of the Simmons Chapter of the Society of American Archivists. She previously attended Oberlin College, where she received her bachelor's degree in musical studies and ethnomusicology.

Samantha Strain is an information professional working as a librarian and a communications and knowledge management specialist at the U.S. Department of Transportation's Volpe National Transportation Systems Center. She also works as a volunteer processing and outreach archivist for The History Project in Boston. Previously, she worked as a project archivist for GLBTQ Legal Advocates & Defenders. She received her MLIS from Simmons in 2018.

Lily Troia is an academic librarian and archivist currently working as an engagement manager at Altmetric. In 2016 she received her MLIS from Simmons, where she was active in student chapters of professional organizations such as the Association of Moving Image Archivists and the Library and Information Sciences Student Association. She has also worked as a project copyright assistant at HarvardX and as a digital services librarian at the College of William & Mary.

Jaye Weatherburn is based in the Digital Scholarship team in Scholarly Services at the University of Melbourne, working to improve and support data stewardship and digital preservation capability. She was an editorial assistant for the *Australian Library Journal* (2014–2016) and is coauthor of *Preserving Digital Materials*, 3rd ed. (2018). She holds a master's in information management and a diploma in professional writing and editing from RMIT University and a bachelor's in film and television from the Victorian College of the Arts (University of Melbourne).